Eyewitness
WATER

Sources of water

Strong electrical attraction

Weak electrical attraction

Oxygen atom

Hydrogen atom

Water molecules

Snake hatching from its egg

Bottled water

Colored solution

Sea anemone

Model of Chinese farmers irrigating land

Snowflake under
the microscope

Eyewitness
WATER

Written by
JOHN WOODWARD

Drop of water

DK Publishing

Seedlings in a
hydroponic solution

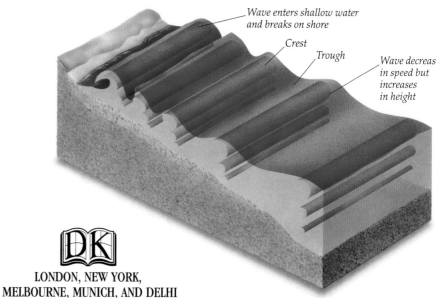

*Wave enters shallow water
and breaks on shore*

Crest

Trough

*Wave decreas
in speed but
increases
in height*

Waves moving toward
the shore

Sea slug

DK

**LONDON, NEW YORK,
MELBOURNE, MUNICH, AND DELHI**

Consultant Professor Dorrik Stow
Project editor Margaret Hynes
Senior editor Rob Houston
Senior art editor Alison Gardner
Managing editor Camilla Hallinan
Managing art editor Owen Peyton Jones
Art director Martin Wilson
Associate publisher Andrew Macintyre
Picture researcher Louise Thomas
Senior production editor Vivianne Ridgeway
Senior production controller Pip Tinsley
Jacket designer Andy Smith

DK DELHI
Design Manager Romi Chakraborty
Designer Ivy Roy
Senior DTP coordinator Sunil Sharma

Model of a
sea-going raft

First published in the United States in 2009 by
DK Publishing, 375 Hudson Street, New York, New York 10014

Copyright © 2009 Dorling Kindersley Limited

09 10 11 12 13 10 9 8 7 6 5 4 3 2 1
ED742 – 01/09

A catalog record for this book is available from the Library of Congress.

ISBN 978-0-7566-4537-3 (HC); 978-0-7566-4538-0 (ALB)

Color reproduction by Colourscan, Singapore.
Printed and bound by Toppan Printing Co. (Shenzen) Ltd., China.

Discover more at
www.dk.com

Fishing hooks
with fly lures

Broad Street
water pump,
London, UK

Plastic duck

Contents

Model of a submersible

Watery world

WATER IS THE MOST IMPORTANT FEATURE of our planet. A simple combination of hydrogen and oxygen, water is probably common throughout the universe, but mainly in the form of ice or water vapor. Both of these are known to occur throughout the solar system, but liquid water seems to be very rare because it can exist only within a limited temperature range. This liquid water is vital to all living organisms, from the simplest microbe to the most complex animal, so it is fundamental to the existence of the whole web of life, humanity, and civilization. Without water, Earth would be a sterile ball of rock.

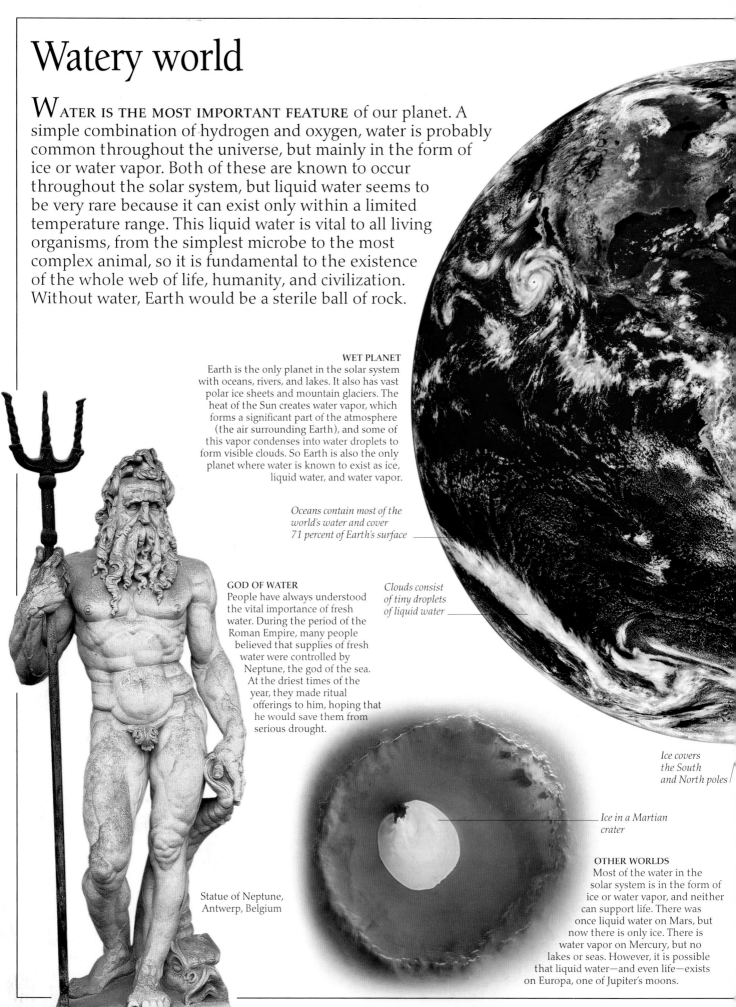

WET PLANET
Earth is the only planet in the solar system with oceans, rivers, and lakes. It also has vast polar ice sheets and mountain glaciers. The heat of the Sun creates water vapor, which forms a significant part of the atmosphere (the air surrounding Earth), and some of this vapor condenses into water droplets to form visible clouds. So Earth is also the only planet where water is known to exist as ice, liquid water, and water vapor.

Oceans contain most of the world's water and cover 71 percent of Earth's surface

GOD OF WATER
People have always understood the vital importance of fresh water. During the period of the Roman Empire, many people believed that supplies of fresh water were controlled by Neptune, the god of the sea. At the driest times of the year, they made ritual offerings to him, hoping that he would save them from serious drought.

Clouds consist of tiny droplets of liquid water

Ice covers the South and North poles

Ice in a Martian crater

Statue of Neptune, Antwerp, Belgium

OTHER WORLDS
Most of the water in the solar system is in the form of ice or water vapor, and neither can support life. There was once liquid water on Mars, but now there is only ice. There is water vapor on Mercury, but no lakes or seas. However, it is possible that liquid water—and even life—exists on Europa, one of Jupiter's moons.

6

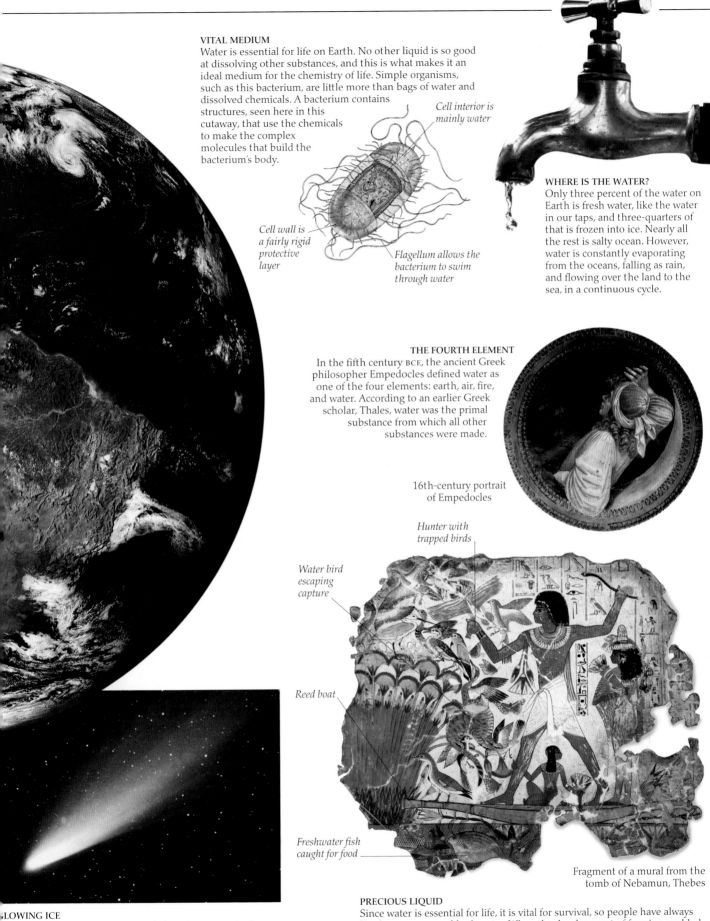

VITAL MEDIUM
Water is essential for life on Earth. No other liquid is so good at dissolving other substances, and this is what makes it an ideal medium for the chemistry of life. Simple organisms, such as this bacterium, are little more than bags of water and dissolved chemicals. A bacterium contains structures, seen here in this cutaway, that use the chemicals to make the complex molecules that build the bacterium's body.

Cell interior is mainly water

Cell wall is a fairly rigid protective layer

Flagellum allows the bacterium to swim through water

WHERE IS THE WATER?
Only three percent of the water on Earth is fresh water, like the water in our taps, and three-quarters of that is frozen into ice. Nearly all the rest is salty ocean. However, water is constantly evaporating from the oceans, falling as rain, and flowing over the land to the sea, in a continuous cycle.

THE FOURTH ELEMENT
In the fifth century BCE, the ancient Greek philosopher Empedocles defined water as one of the four elements: earth, air, fire, and water. According to an earlier Greek scholar, Thales, water was the primal substance from which all other substances were made.

16th-century portrait of Empedocles

Hunter with trapped birds

Water bird escaping capture

Reed boat

Freshwater fish caught for food

Fragment of a mural from the tomb of Nebamun, Thebes

LOWING ICE
Vater is constantly hurtling around the solar system in the orm of comets—"dirty snowballs" of ice and dust with longated orbits that swerve around the Sun before vanishing eyond the outer planets. They appear for a few days in the ight sky, trailing clouds of glowing debris, then fade away.

PRECIOUS LIQUID
Since water is essential for life, it is vital for survival, so people have always lived near sources of fresh water. When the development of farming enabled people to build the first cities, most of these were sited by reliable water sources. The earliest civilizations were based on great rivers like the Euphrates, Tigris, Nile, and Yellow rivers. This wall painting dating from about 3,400 years ago shows an Egyptian hunter in the Nile marshes.

Water and history

SINCE WATER IS VITAL TO OUR SURVIVAL, it has always played a pivotal role in human history. Most cities and other settlements were sited by sources of fresh water, especially in dry regions. But water has also been used for travel—along rivers, coasts, and eventually out of sight of land. For much of history overland travel could be very difficul so despite the dangers on the water it was often easier to travel by boat. Many great cities developed on natural harbors and rivers that were large enough for ships to travel on them. These cities became wealthy through maritime trade. Having learned how to cross oceans, people were then able to visit and colonize distant lands.

Model of a sea-going raft

Sail harnesses the power of the wind

Mast made from light, springy lumber

Simple shelter

Logs lashed together

RAFTS AND DUGOUTS
The first water craft were built from logs, either hollowed out as canoes or lashed together as rafts. Using such craft, people were able to spread along rivers and even along coasts. This led to the earliest ocean crossings by the brave people who colonized Australia from Indonesia, some 50,000 years ago.

FINDING THE WAY
At first sailors relied on local knowledge to find their way and avoid dangerous waters. But over time they depended increasingly on charts such as this 17th-century map of northern Europe. Yet these were no use without some way of finding a ship's position at sea. The invention of the compass for finding magnetic north, the sextant for navigation by the Sun and stars, and the development of clocks that could give accurate times for use in calculating longitude, all made seafaring much safer.

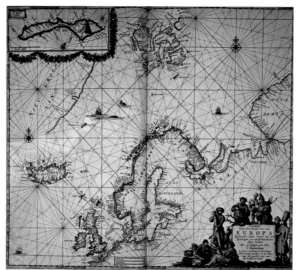

Statue of James Cook (1728–1779)

TRADING CITIES
Access to trading routes brought wealth to many coastal and river settlements. Some developed into spectacular cities such as Venice, Shanghai, and New York. Merchants, including the 14th-century Venetian explorer Marco Polo, brought exotic goods, such as this Chinese porcelain vase, back from distant lands.

Marco Polo sets sail from Venice

Chinese vase

VOYAGES OF DISCOVERY
As knowledge of the oceans and how to cross them grew, seafarers became more ambitious. Explorers such as the English sailor James Cook—here commemorated by a statue in Hawaii, where he was killed—made scientific expeditions to map all the world's oceans, continents, and islands.

Cinnamon

Cloves

Cardamom

Nutmeg

SPICE ISLANDS
In the 16th and 17th centuries the spice islands of the East Indies were the only sources of valuable products such as nutmeg and cloves. European traders fought for control over these islands. The first voyage around the world, led by the Portuguese sailor Ferdinand Magellan in 1519–1523, originated as a plan to reach the islands by crossing the Pacific rather than the usual route across the Indian Ocean.

RIDING THE WINDS
In the 19th and early 20th centuries huge sailing ships crossed oceans to bring tea from China and grain from Australia. They sailed in some of the stormiest waters on Earth, but the stronger the winds, the faster the passage. The fastest ships raced each other to be the first home—a tradition that is kept alive by the around-the-world yacht races of today.

Danmark, a Danish merchant navy training ship, was built in 1933

Sharp cutlass

Single-shot pistol

PIRACY
Trading ships packed with rich cargo were a constant temptation to pirates, who were often sea captains who had turned to crime. English pirate Edward Teach, or "Blackbeard," was notorious for his terrifying appearance, designed to make his victims surrender without a fight.

MASS MIGRATION
The seas have offered a migration route for people from the earliest times, but regular ships to the Americas and Australia from the mid-18th century permitted mass migrations of people such as these refugees from the Irish famine in the 1840s. Immigrants often traveled in squalid conditions on badly maintained vessels, and many died at sea.

What is water?

WE ARE ALL SO USED TO WATER that we barely notice its unusual nature. Most of us think of water as a flowing, splashing liquid, but it is also the only natural substance that is found in all three states—liquid, solid (ice), and gas (water vapor)—at the temperatures normally found on Earth. When it turns into ice it actually expands, or gets bigger, unlike all other substances that take up less space when they freeze. Water may also clump together in drops instead of spreading out in thin layers, and it forms elastic films at its surface that can support the weight of small animals. All these properties can be explained by water's chemical makeup.

Strong electrical attraction between atoms

Weak electrical attraction between molecules

Oxygen atom

Hydrogen atom

TRIANGULAR MOLECULES
Water is a mass of molecules, each with two hydrogen atoms and one oxygen atom. The atoms are held together by electrical charges that make them form a triangle. The charges also make the molecules stick to one another like tiny triangular magnets to form liquid water.

Insect's weight dimples surface film

SURFACE TENSION
The tendency of liquid water molecules to stick to one another is stronger at the surface of a pool, at the boundary between water and air. It makes the surface molecules cling together to form an elastic film known as surface tension. The film is strong enough to bear the weight of small aquatic animals, such as this water strider.

WATER DROPS
The surface tension around a small amount of airborne water acts like an elastic envelope, pulling the water into a spherical drop like this one. A drop that lands on a surface that repels water, such as a hairy leaf, has a similar spherical form because the envelope of surface tension is not distorted by the water sticking to the leaf. But water molecules can also stick to other materials such as glass, so the surface tension breaks down and the drop spreads out in a thin layer.

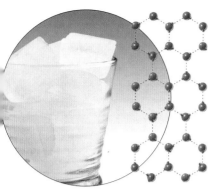

OLID ICE
When water freezes, the molecules lock nto an open structure that forms hexagonal e crystals. The molecules are farther apart han they are in the liquid phase, so water xpands as it freezes. This means that ice is ot as dense as water, which is why it floats.

LIQUID WATER
When ice melts, the regular structure of the molecules in the ice crystals collapses. The molecules move closer to each other, attracted by the electrical forces that hold them together. But they can still move around, which is why water is liquid.

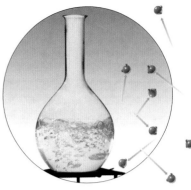

WATER VAPOR
The molecules in liquid water are always moving. If the water is heated, this gives the molecules more energy, so they move faster. Eventually they may move fast enough to break free and burst into the air to become an invisible gas, called water vapor.

REEZING POINT
Vater freezes at 32°F (0°C), but only if is pure. Impurities such as dissolved lt lower its freezing point, which is hy spreading salt on winter roads duces the risk of ice forming. The salt seawater causes this water to freeze a lower temperature than fresh ater, at roughly 28.8°F (−1.8°C).

Visible steam consists of tiny water droplets

BOILING POINT
At sea level, water boils at 212°F (100°C). But on mountains where the atmospheric pressure is lower, water evaporates more easily and boils at a lower temperature. This allows people in Tibet to drink their tea while it is still boiling. Higher pressure raises boiling point, enabling water in a pressure cooker to be "superheated" to 248°F (120°C) or more.

HEAVY WATER
Water is made of two gases, so it is surprising that a bucket of water is so heavy. It is heavy because all the molecules cling together tightly, making it dense. Its density enables water to support less dense liquids such as oil, or materials that contain air spaces, such as wood.

Oil floats on water

Water is heavier than oil

LIQUID, SOLID, GAS
These icy-furred macaques in a hot pool are experiencing all three phases of water at once. This is possible because ice forms easily in the cold air, and water does not need to reach boiling point for some of its molecules to escape and form water vapor.

Fresh and saltwater

WATER IS RARELY PURE. As it flows from one place to another it carries a wide range of substances with it. This is because the atoms of chemicals dissolve, or disperse, in water more easily than in any other liquid. The dissolved chemicals form a liquid called a solution. Many different liquids, gases, and solids can form solutions. The ocean is a solution of minerals that make it taste salty. Some dissolved minerals make acids and alkalis, which are chemicals that can cause strong reactions. Water also carries small particles that do not dissolve. These mixtures are called suspensions.

Limescale on kettle element

HARD AND SOFT
Rainwater flowing over rocks such as limestone dissolves minerals called carbonates. If this "hard water" is boiled, the carbonates are deposited in the kettle as limescale. Rainwater that flows over insoluble rock such as granite or sandstone is "soft water" that does not cause limescale.

CLEAR SOLUTION
Many solutions of chemicals in water are colorless. A saltwater solution looks just like pure water, and the difference is only obvious from the scent or taste. However, the salt does increase the density of the water.

COLORED SOLUTION
If water dissolves chemicals that are colored, they can form a colored solution. But since the atoms or ions of the original substance are completely dispersed, the solution is transparent, like pure water.

SUSPENSION
Water can also support small particles or droplets without dissolving them. This muddy water is a suspension of soil particles. The particles are too small to see when mixed. They are what makes the water cloudy.

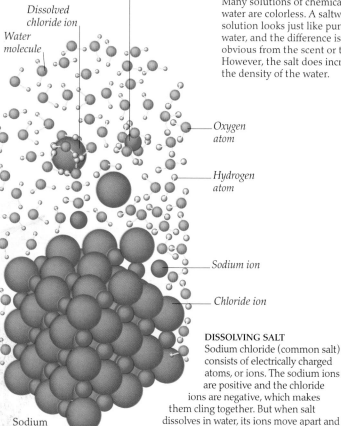

Dissolved sodium ion

Dissolved chloride ion

Water molecule

Oxygen atom

Hydrogen atom

Sodium ion

Chloride ion

Sodium chloride crystal

DISSOLVING SALT
Sodium chloride (common salt) consists of electrically charged atoms, or ions. The sodium ions are positive and the chloride ions are negative, which makes them cling together. But when salt dissolves in water, its ions move apart and form "hydrated ions," with each former salt ion clinging to water molecules.

SALT CRYSTALS
The bond holding a water molecule together is stronger than the bond that links it to a salt ion. If salt water evaporates, the water-salt bonds break while the water molecules float away as pure water vapor. If all the water evaporates, the salt ions join up to form white salt crystals like these.

ACID AND ALKALINE
Acidic rainwater is dissolving this limestone statue. Rainwater is slightly acid because it combines with carbon dioxide in the air to form a weak carbonic acid. If it dissolves an alkaline rock such as limestone, this turns the water slightly alkaline. So soft water is faintly acid but hard water is mildly alkaline.

ATMOSPHERIC GASES
Water dissolves oxygen as well as carbon dioxide from the air. The colder the water, the more oxygen it can contain. All living organisms depend on supplies of oxygen and carbon dioxide, so this ability of water to dissolve atmospheric gases is vital to aquatic plant and animal life.

Oxygen produced by the plant will dissolve in water

SYMBOL OF PURITY
Although water is rarely pure, it has been seen as an emblem of purity for thousands of years. Many religions have purification rituals involving water, often in the form of symbolic washing—as in baptismal rites. Here a devout Hindu bathes in the sacred waters of the Ganges in India, an act that is believed to wash away sins and help gain salvation.

ESSENTIAL NUTRIENTS
The fertilizers used by farmers are made up of nitrates, phosphates, potassium, and other nutrients that plants need to grow. The plants can absorb them only if they are dissolved in water. Since animals depend on plant tissue for food, these nutrient solutions are essential to all life.

Light, sound, and pressure

WATER IS PHYSICALLY VERY DIFFERENT from air. Water absorbs light and heat, so they do not penetrate far through deep water, yet it is amazingly efficient at transmitting sound because of its great density compared to air. Water's density makes it heavy, so deep water exerts immense pressure. These properties make water an alien environment for us, even though we need it to survive. But the physical properties of water affect life on land too, because the oceans absorb a lot of the Sun's heat energy and this has a big influence on climate.

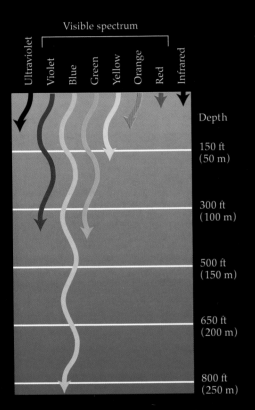

Visible spectrum

Ultraviolet | Violet | Blue | Green | Yellow | Orange | Red | Infrared

Depth

150 ft (50 m)

300 ft (100 m)

500 ft (150 m)

650 ft (200 m)

800 ft (250 m)

LIGHT FILTER
White sunlight contains all the colors of the spectrum. When sunlight shines into deep water, some colors are absorbed or filtered out, along with invisible infrared and ultraviolet, leaving only blue. Blue light penetrates much more deeply before being absorbed, leaving darkness.

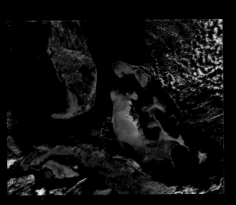

BLUE WATER
Since blue light penetrates most deeply into water, everything in the ocean appears blue below a certain depth. Some of this blue light is scattered back to the surface, which is why oceans look blue from space. Seawater is also blue when seen from sea level, and shallow beds of white sand appear turquoise.

Sunlit zone

Twilight zone

Dark zone

LIGHT ZONES
In the oceans, and in deep lakes, the absorption of sunlight creates distinct light zones. Just below the surface lies the sunlit zone, where there is enough light for aquatic plants and algae. In clear, tropical water this zone can be up to about 650 ft (200 m) deep. Deeper than the sunlit zone there is just dim blue light, creating the twilight zone to depths of up to 3,000 ft (900 m). The region below this receives no sunlight at all, so it is known as the dark zone. In murky, muddy conditions the zones occur in much shallower water.

Line of sensory pores runs along the side of the fish

PRESSURE SENSE
Aquatic animals are aware of each other's movements because the water transmits the loc changes of pressure that the movements cause. Fish pick up the changes with their pressure-sensitive lateral line system, and this enables shoals to swim in perfectly coordinated formatio

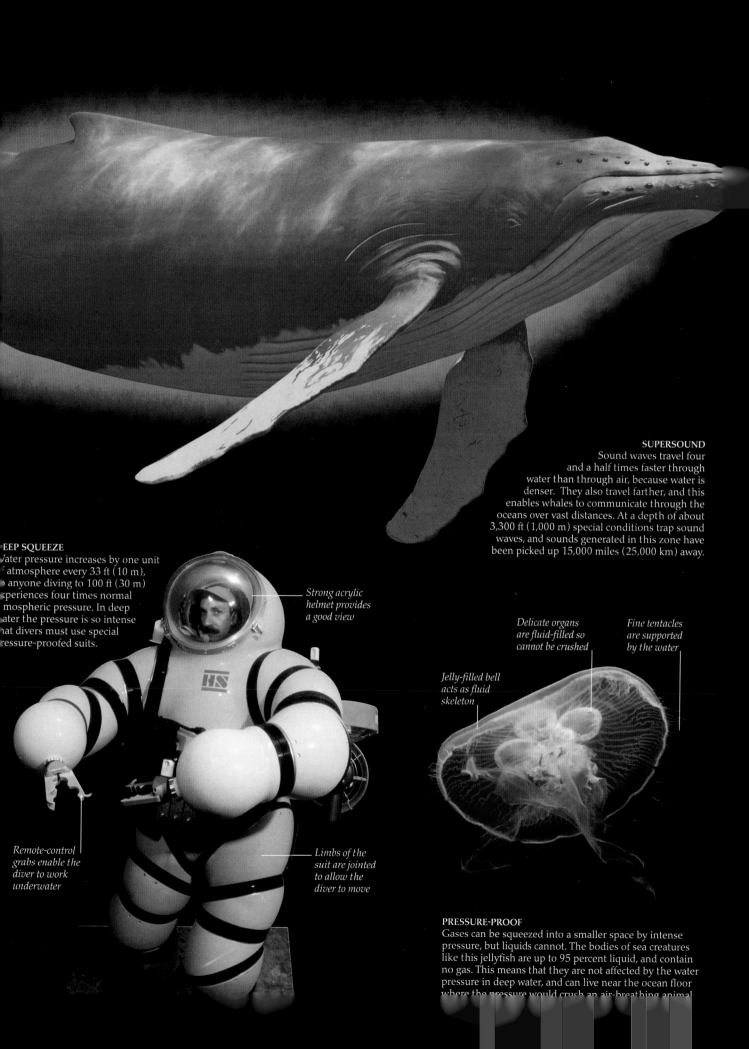

SUPERSOUND
Sound waves travel four and a half times faster through water than through air, because water is denser. They also travel farther, and this enables whales to communicate through the oceans over vast distances. At a depth of about 3,300 ft (1,000 m) special conditions trap sound waves, and sounds generated in this zone have been picked up 15,000 miles (25,000 km) away.

DEEP SQUEEZE
Water pressure increases by one unit of atmosphere every 33 ft (10 m), so anyone diving to 100 ft (30 m) experiences four times normal atmospheric pressure. In deep water the pressure is so intense that divers must use special pressure-proofed suits.

Strong acrylic helmet provides a good view

Remote-control grabs enable the diver to work underwater

Limbs of the suit are jointed to allow the diver to move

Delicate organs are fluid-filled so cannot be crushed

Fine tentacles are supported by the water

Jelly-filled bell acts as fluid skeleton

PRESSURE-PROOF
Gases can be squeezed into a smaller space by intense pressure, but liquids cannot. The bodies of sea creatures like this jellyfish are up to 95 percent liquid, and contain no gas. This means that they are not affected by the water pressure in deep water, and can live near the ocean floor where the pressure would crush an air-breathing animal.

Oceans and seas

VOLCANIC WATER
Most of the water on Earth was probably released as water vapor by massive volcanoes some 4.2 billion years ago. It originally formed part of the atmosphere, but as the planet cooled the vapor condensed into rain that poured down to create a global ocean.

Oceans COVER MORE THAN TWO-THIRDS of the planet, to an average depth of 2½ miles (3.8 km), and contain 97 percent of the world's water. The first ocean formed very early in Earth's history. The oldest known rocks, which are at least 4 billion years old, have features that show they originally formed on an ocean floor. This means that oceans probably existed before the continents and may have covered the whole globe. This ocean was split up by continents forming from volcanic eruptions and slowly drifting around the world on the moving plates of Earth's crust—a process that depends on water seeping through the ocean floors and making the rocks slide more easily.

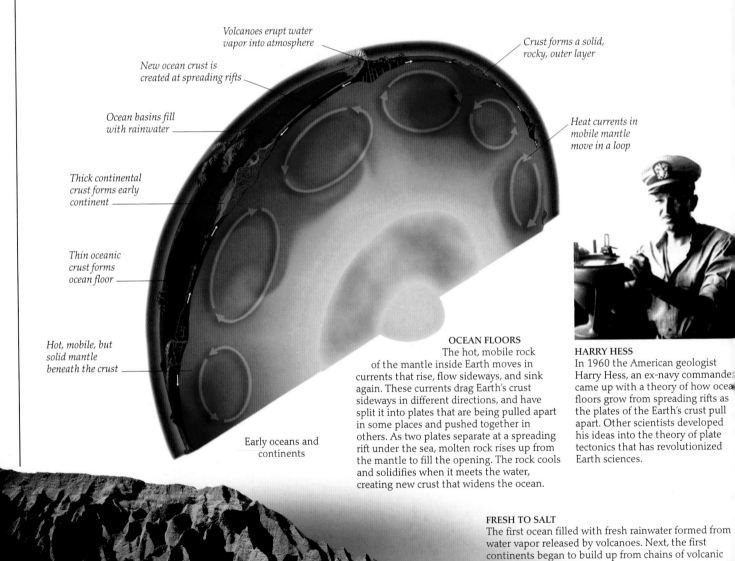

Volcanoes erupt water vapor into atmosphere

New ocean crust is created at spreading rifts

Ocean basins fill with rainwater

Thick continental crust forms early continent

Thin oceanic crust forms ocean floor

Hot, mobile, but solid mantle beneath the crust

Crust forms a solid, rocky, outer layer

Heat currents in mobile mantle move in a loop

Early oceans and continents

OCEAN FLOORS
The hot, mobile rock of the mantle inside Earth moves in currents that rise, flow sideways, and sink again. These currents drag Earth's crust sideways in different directions, and have split it into plates that are being pulled apart in some places and pushed together in others. As two plates separate at a spreading rift under the sea, molten rock rises up from the mantle to fill the opening. The rock cools and solidifies when it meets the water, creating new crust that widens the ocean.

HARRY HESS
In 1960 the American geologist Harry Hess, an ex-navy commander, came up with a theory of how ocean floors grow from spreading rifts as the plates of the Earth's crust pull apart. Other scientists developed his ideas into the theory of plate tectonics that has revolutionized Earth sciences.

FRESH TO SALT
The first ocean filled with fresh rainwater formed from water vapor released by volcanoes. Next, the first continents began to build up from chains of volcanic islands. Erosion by heavy rain washed mineral salts off the new land and into the ocean, making it salty for the first time. The deep gullies in the sides of this volcanic island show that this is still happening. Other agents—mainly living organisms—remove salt and store it in seafloor sediments, so the salt content of the oceans has stabilized

THE ROLE OF WATER

Water seeping through the ocean floors lowers the melting point of the hot rock of Earth's mantle, just as salt lowers the melting point of ice. This turns the rock into molten basalt, like this lava from a Hawaiian volcano. The molten rock acts like oil, enabling the great plates of the Earth's crust to slide around the globe. Without water, there might be no plate tectonics, and Earth would look very different.

SHALLOW SEAS

Coastal waters are much shallower than open oceans because they cover the submerged edge of a continent—the continental shelf. This extends to the continental slope, which descends to the true ocean floor. At times of low sea level in the past, such as during ice ages, many continental shelves were dry land.

Coast

Continental shelf

Continental slope

Continental crust

Oceanic crust

Deep ocean floor

Side thruster aids steering

Lifting point for hoisting onto mother ship

Strong titanium sphere inside hull protects crew

Ifremer

nautile

Ifremer nautile

Lights and cameras

EXPLORING THE DEEP

Most of what we know about the ocean floors has been discovered using remote sensing techniques such as sonar (depth sounding), magnetic surveys, gravity measurements, and submarine earthquake detection. But deepwater submersibles, such as *Nautile*, now allow scientists to visit the ocean floor and see it for themselves.

Main thruster provides power

Ocean layers and currents

OCEAN WATER DOES NOT ALL LOOK THE SAME. The blue water of the warm tropics (around the equator) is very different from the gray-green of cold coastal seas, or the drifting pack ice of polar oceans. These differences are caused by the heat of the Sun, which warms the surface waters of tropical oceans far more than those nearer the poles, and creates layers of warm and cold water at different depths. It also generates the global air movements that cause winds, and these interact with the spinning of the planet to drive ocean surface currents. The surface currents are linked to deepwater currents in a system that carries ocean water all around the world, redistributing heat and helping to reduce extremes of temperature. Ocean currents also transport the dissolved gases and nutrients that are essential to oceanic life.

90°F — 32°C
— 30°C
70°F — 20°C
50°F — 10°C
30°F — 0°C

Constantly warm water in Caribbean Sea, where the tropical sunshine is more intense

North America

South America

SURFACE WATERS
Sunlight warms the ocean surface, especially in the tropics where the sunshine is more intense. But the warmth does not penetrate very deeply. Surface water absorbs the heat to form a warm surface layer. This expands and becomes less dense, so it floats on the denser, heavier cold water. These two layers are separated by a transition zone called the thermocline.

INVISIBLE BARRIER
In cold oceans seasonal storms tend to break down the thermocline. This allows surface waters to mix with the cold, nutrient-rich water from below. The nutrients encourage plankton growth, turning the water cloudy green. In most warm oceans the thermocline stops nutrient-rich water reaching the surface, so tropical waters are usually clear blue.

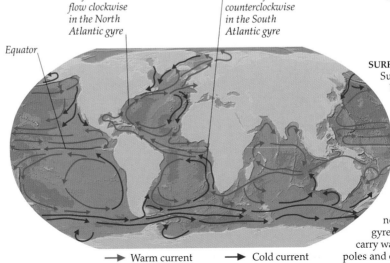

Surface currents flow clockwise in the North Atlantic gyre

Currents flow counterclockwise in the South Atlantic gyre

Equator

SURFACE CURRENTS
Surface currents are driven by the winds, which blow toward the west near the equator, and toward the east in temperate zones. The winds tend to drag the surface waters of the oceans with them, creating huge clockwise circular currents, or gyres, in the north, and anticlockwise gyres in the south. These carry warm water toward the poles and cold water to the tropics

→ Warm current   → Cold current

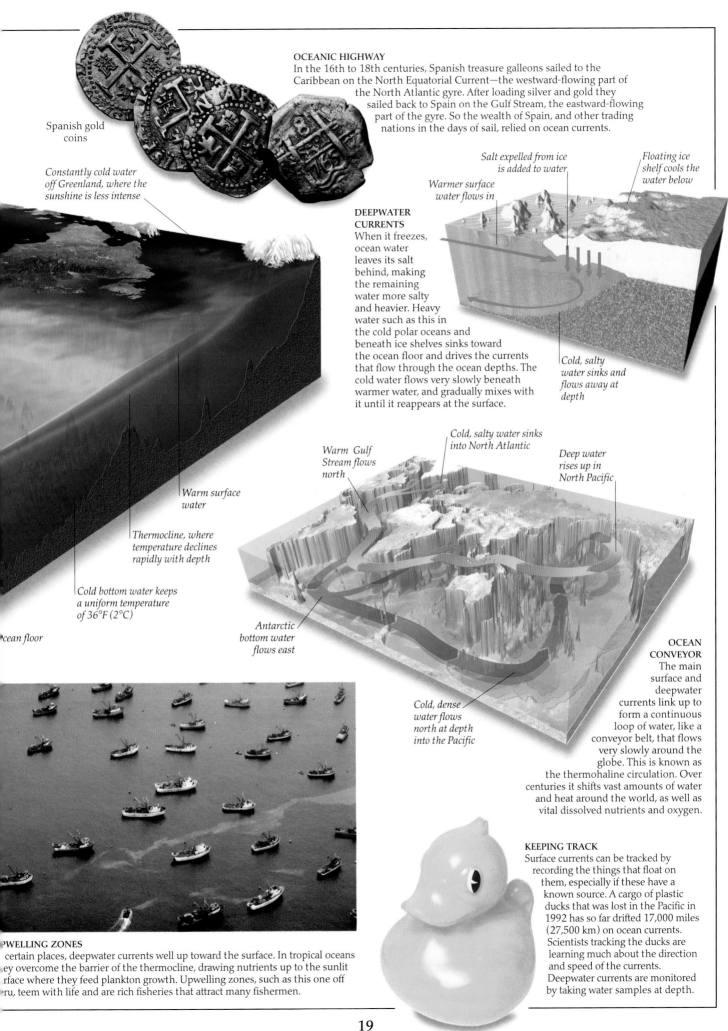

Spanish gold
coins

OCEANIC HIGHWAY
In the 16th to 18th centuries, Spanish treasure galleons sailed to the
Caribbean on the North Equatorial Current—the westward-flowing part of
the North Atlantic gyre. After loading silver and gold they
sailed back to Spain on the Gulf Stream, the eastward-flowing
part of the gyre. So the wealth of Spain, and other trading
nations in the days of sail, relied on ocean currents.

*Constantly cold water
off Greenland, where the
sunshine is less intense*

*Salt expelled from ice
is added to water*

*Floating ice
shelf cools the
water below*

*Warmer surface
water flows in*

**DEEPWATER
CURRENTS**
When it freezes,
ocean water
leaves its salt
behind, making
the remaining
water more salty
and heavier. Heavy
water such as this in
the cold polar oceans and
beneath ice shelves sinks toward
the ocean floor and drives the currents
that flow through the ocean depths. The
cold water flows very slowly beneath
warmer water, and gradually mixes with
it until it reappears at the surface.

*Cold, salty
water sinks and
flows away at
depth*

*Warm surface
water*

*Thermocline, where
temperature declines
rapidly with depth*

*Cold bottom water keeps
a uniform temperature
of 36°F (2°C)*

Ocean floor

*Warm Gulf
Stream flows
north*

*Cold, salty water sinks
into North Atlantic*

*Deep water
rises up in
North Pacific*

*Antarctic
bottom water
flows east*

*Cold, dense
water flows
north at depth
into the Pacific*

**OCEAN
CONVEYOR**
The main
surface and
deepwater
currents link up to
form a continuous
loop of water, like a
conveyor belt, that flows
very slowly around the
globe. This is known as
the thermohaline circulation. Over
centuries it shifts vast amounts of water
and heat around the world, as well as
vital dissolved nutrients and oxygen.

KEEPING TRACK
Surface currents can be tracked by
recording the things that float on
them, especially if these have a
known source. A cargo of plastic
ducks that was lost in the Pacific in
1992 has so far drifted 17,000 miles
(27,500 km) on ocean currents.
Scientists tracking the ducks are
learning much about the direction
and speed of the currents.
Deepwater currents are monitored
by taking water samples at depth.

UPWELLING ZONES
In certain places, deepwater currents well up toward the surface. In tropical oceans
they overcome the barrier of the thermocline, drawing nutrients up to the sunlit
surface where they feed plankton growth. Upwelling zones, such as this one off
Peru, teem with life and are rich fisheries that attract many fishermen.

Waves and tides

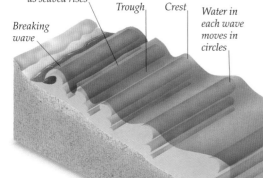

Wave gets higher as seabed rises

Breaking wave

Trough

Crest

Water in each wave moves in circles

THE WINDS THAT DRIVE OCEAN CURRENTS also whip up waves. Ocean waves are ripples of energy. Unlike currents, they do not move water any great distance, but as they move, they carry energy forward through the ocean. Waves can be very destructive, because of their height—which can be enough to overwhelm even big ships—and because of the weight of water that crashes forward when they break on the shore. By contrast the tides that rise and fall every day shift masses of seawater along coastlines, creating tidal streams that can flow much faster than ocean currents. Where they flow through narrow channels and around headlands they can create dangerous races and whirlpools.

WIND AND WAVES
When wind blows over the ocean's surface, it creates waves of energy that travel through the water in a series of crests (high points) and troughs (low points). Each wave lifts water particles around in circles. As waves approach a shore, the circulation of water at the bottom of the wave is slowed by the seabed and the top spills over.

ROGUE WAVES
Out at sea, two wave systems may meet. The waves either cancel each other out or combine to create huge rogue waves up to 100 ft (30 m) high. Such waves are big enough to engulf big ships and even sink them. Here a scene from the film *The Perfect Storm* shows a fishing boat about to be overwhelmed.

DESTRUCTIVE FORCE
When a wave reaches shallow water it gets shorter and steeper until its crest topples forward and breaks. All its energy then smashes on the shore, forcing water into cracks in exposed rock and blowing the rock apart by hydraulic pressure. The water also picks up rock fragments and smashes them against exposed shores to speed up erosion.

BEACH BUILDING
All the rocky debris created by wave action is broken into smaller fragments. As these are tumbled in the surf they are reduced to pebbles and sand. These are swept along the shore to places where the waves are less violent and do not carry them back out to sea. The big stones are dropped first to form shingle banks, but finer particles are carried to more sheltered parts of the coast where they form beaches of grit or sand.

Large pebbles are soon dropped by waves

Small pebbles are carried further

Grit forms coarse-grained beaches

Sand creates beaches in bays with calmer water

Earthquake causes uplift / seafloor

Water suddenly elevated

Wave is long but low in deep ocean

Wave becomes tall and destructive in shallow water

EARTH

Moon's gravity creates a tidal bulge

MOON

Second tidal bulge forms on the other side of Earth

Combined tidal bulges

Earth spins while its tidal bulges stay aligned with the Moon

TSUNAMIS
The most notorious waves are tsunamis, which are triggered by submarine earthquakes and explosive eruptions of volcanic islands. Tsunamis have relatively low crests out at sea, which are a long way apart, but they build up into very high waves with deep troughs as they approach the shore. They can cause immense damage as they sweep inland, as in 2004 when the Asian Tsunami killed about 300,000 people.

LOCAL TIDES
On most coasts the tide rises and falls twice a day, leaving boats like these stranded at low tide. But local geography, such as the shape of the coast or the seabed, can reduce this to once a day, or even eliminate tides altogether. It can also concentrate the tidal flow to cause huge tides, and this may create dangerously fast local currents.

HIGH AND LOW TIDES
Tides are caused by the gravity of the Moon stretching Earth's oceans into an oval shape because its pull is strongest on the side of Earth facing the Moon and weakest on the opposite side. This makes tidal bulges form on both sides of the globe. As the Earth spins on its axis most coastal localities pass through both tidal bulges every day, so they experience two high tides and two low tides. The Sun's gravity also plays a role. If the Sun pulls in the same direction as the Moon, the tides are more extreme.

RIDING THE WAVES
The farther waves travel while still being blown by the wind, the bigger they get. This means that persistent strong winds over broad oceans like the Pacific can generate huge waves. Where these break on oceanic islands, such as Hawaii, they provide surfers with the best wave-riding conditions on Earth.

Water and weather

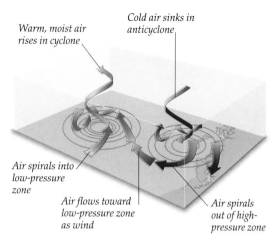

Warm, moist air rises in cyclone

Cold air sinks in anticyclone

Air spirals into low-pressure zone

Air flows toward low-pressure zone as wind

Air spirals out of high-pressure zone

HEAT AND PRESSURE
Sun-warmed water evaporates and rises into the air as water vapor. The warm air spirals upward, carrying the water vapor with it. Rising warm air creates low-pressure areas called cyclones. Meanwhile, cool air may be sinking in a nearby high-pressure zone, or anticyclone. Air moves from higher to lower pressure, and we feel this as wind. High pressure usually brings dry, fine weather, and low pressure usually brings rain.

WATER IS A VITAL ELEMENT OF THE WEATHER. The water vapor that evaporates from oceans, lakes, rivers, and forest condenses and often freezes to form the clouds, rain, and snow that are such an obvious feature of weather systems. But the processes of evaporation and condensation that lead to rainfall and snowfall also absorb and release energy that is converted into wind. The most extreme forms of weather, such as thunderstorms and hurricanes, are largely driven by energy stored and released in this way. So water does not just provide us with rain—it also helps power the whole weather machine.

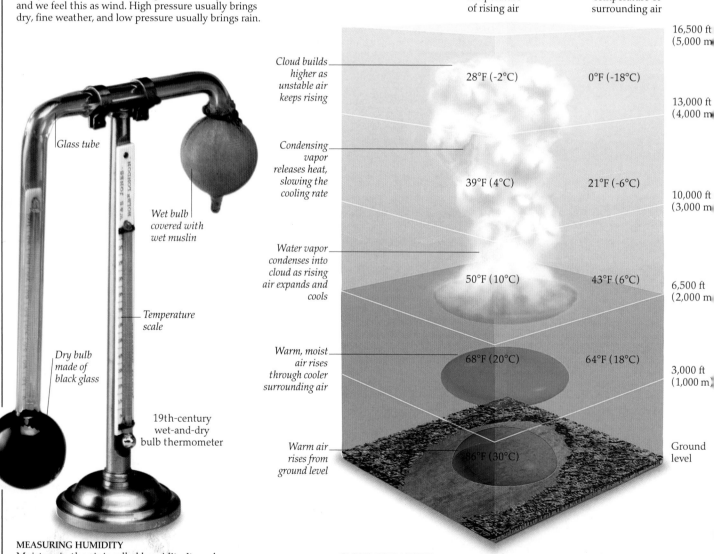

Temperature of rising air | Temperature of surrounding air

Cloud builds higher as unstable air keeps rising — 28°F (-2°C) — 0°F (-18°C) — 16,500 ft (5,000 m)

13,000 ft (4,000 m)

Condensing vapor releases heat, slowing the cooling rate — 39°F (4°C) — 21°F (-6°C) — 10,000 ft (3,000 m)

Water vapor condenses into cloud as rising air expands and cools — 50°F (10°C) — 43°F (6°C) — 6,500 ft (2,000 m)

Warm, moist air rises through cooler surrounding air — 68°F (20°C) — 64°F (18°C) — 3,000 ft (1,000 m)

Warm air rises from ground level — 86°F (30°C) — Ground level

Glass tube

Wet bulb covered with wet muslin

Temperature scale

Dry bulb made of black glass

19th-century wet-and-dry bulb thermometer

MEASURING HUMIDITY
Moisture in the air is called humidity. It can be measured with a wet-and-dry bulb thermometer such as this one. The dry bulb is an ordinary thermometer. The wet bulb is surrounded by wet muslin. As this dries out it cools the bulb. The drier the air, the cooler the wet bulb becomes. So the greater the difference in readings between the two bulbs, the lower the humidity.

CLOUD FORMATION
As warm, moist air rises, it expands and cools. The water vapor cools too, and condenses into tiny water droplets that form clouds. The condensation process releases heat that slows the cooling rate, so the air in the cloud is warmer than the surrounding air. The warm air continues to rise, building the cloud higher, until there is no water vapor left, or the rising air becomes cooler than the air surrounding it.

Cirrus
Cirrocumulus
Cirrostratus

High level, above 20,000 ft (6,000 m)

Altocumulus
Altostratus

Middle level, 6,500–20,000 ft (2,000–6,000 m)

Stratocumulus
Stratus

Cumulus
Nimbostratus   Cumulonimbus

Low level, 0–6,500 ft (0–2,000 m)

TYPES OF CLOUDS
There are ten basic types of clouds, with names that indicate their appearance or effect: for example, cirrus (curl), stratus (layer), cumulus (heap), and nimbus (rain). Most occur at either low, medium, or high level, but the colossal cumulonimbus clouds that cause thunderstorms tower up to 10 miles (16 km) in the air.

LUKE HOWARD
The system of naming clouds is based on the cloud classification devised in 1802 by English manufacturing chemist and amateur meteorologist Luke Howard. His *Essay on the Modification of Clouds*, which was published in 1803, was the first scientific study of cloud types. Howard's system proved so simple and effective that it is still used by meteorologists today.

RAIN AND SNOW
Rising and falling air currents inside clouds hurl the tiny cloud droplets around so they collide and form bigger droplets. These may eventually get heavy enough to fall as rain. The same thing happens with the microscopic ice crystals that form high-level clouds, making them stick together to form snowflakes.

Surface of hailstone is typically uneven

HAIL
Raindrops tossed around inside storm clouds can rise to altitudes where they freeze solid. They then fall back, pick up more water, and are hurled upward again. The layers of ice form hailstones that eventually tumble out of the sky. The bigger the cloud, the bigger the hailstones can become.

TORM CLOUDS
Vhere evaporation is intense, masses of water vapor rise, cool, and ondense to form big clouds. This releases heat energy, which warms the air nd makes it rise higher, carrying more water vapor with it. This condenses, eleasing more heat. If there is enough water vapor this can create huge umulonimbus storm clouds. Eventually the weight of water in the cloud uilds up to the point where the rising air currents cannot upport it, and it is released as torrential rain.

URRICANES
he biggest storm clouds row over tropical oceans, here they form deep w-pressure systems hat draw in extremely trong winds. These opical cyclones or urricanes also cause ceanic storm surges at resemble local but tense tsunamis. These n flood low-lying coasts, s in New Orleans in 2005 nd Myanmar (Burma) in 2008.

The water cycle

W ATER VAPOR RISING FROM THE OCEANS forms clouds that are carried over land by weather systems. The clouds spill rain and snow, which form streams, rivers, and glaciers that flow back into the ocean. Even the water that seeps into the ground eventually finds its way back to the sea. This sequence is called the water cycle. When the water evaporates from the oceans it leaves its salt content behind to become pure, fresh water, but as it flows overland it dissolves minerals and other substances which it carries into the sea. From there the cycle starts again.

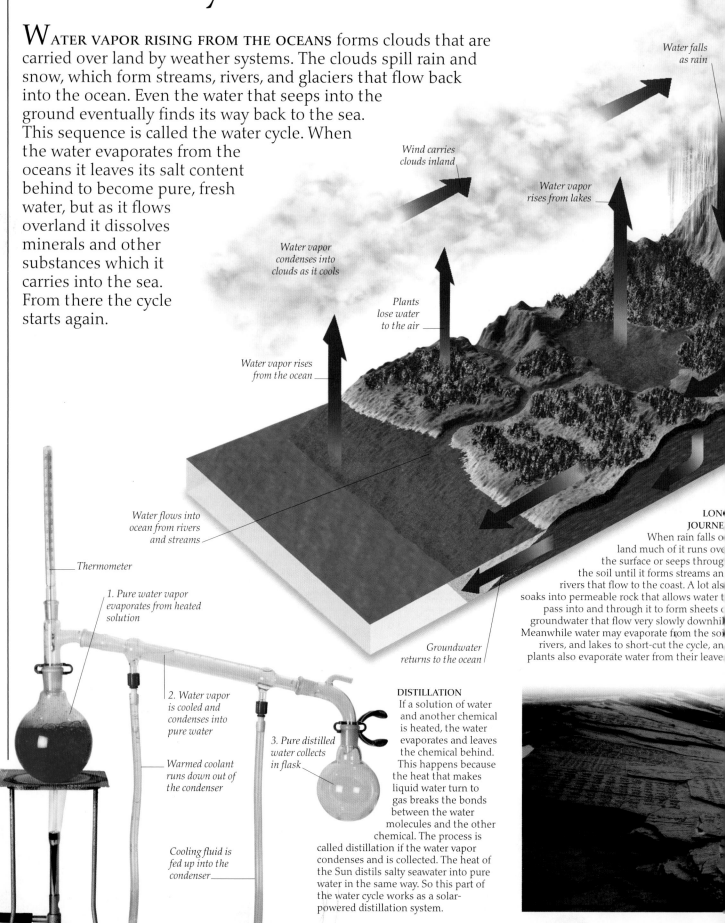

Water falls as rain

Wind carries clouds inland

Water vapor rises from lakes

Water vapor condenses into clouds as it cools

Plants lose water to the air

Water vapor rises from the ocean

Water flows into ocean from rivers and streams

Thermometer

1. Pure water vapor evaporates from heated solution

2. Water vapor is cooled and condenses into pure water

3. Pure distilled water collects in flask

Warmed coolant runs down out of the condenser

Cooling fluid is fed up into the condenser

Groundwater returns to the ocean

LONG JOURNEY
When rain falls on land much of it runs over the surface or seeps through the soil until it forms streams and rivers that flow to the coast. A lot also soaks into permeable rock that allows water to pass into and through it to form sheets of groundwater that flow very slowly downhill. Meanwhile water may evaporate from the soil, rivers, and lakes to short-cut the cycle, and plants also evaporate water from their leaves.

DISTILLATION
If a solution of water and another chemical is heated, the water evaporates and leaves the chemical behind. This happens because the heat that makes liquid water turn to gas breaks the bonds between the water molecules and the other chemical. The process is called distillation if the water vapor condenses and is collected. The heat of the Sun distils salty seawater into pure water in the same way. So this part of the water cycle works as a solar-powered distillation system.

24

Water freezes and
falls as snow

Ice forms
glaciers

Drainage water
seeps into
ground

Rivers and streams
flow off the land

DAYS, YEARS, CENTURIES

Some parts of the water cycle have a fast turnover, such as heavy rain that can drain off a small rocky island within hours of falling. Other parts of the cycle take much longer. For example, groundwater that takes many years to flow back to the sea. Some water that soaks deep into rocks stays there for centuries. Much of the water that falls as snow is compressed into dense blue glacier ice. It is locked up for thousands of years before rejoining the cycle.

SHORT CUT

In hot climates, much of the rain that falls never makes it back to the ocean. In deserts, rainwater evaporates almost as soon as it hits the ground. A lot of the rain that falls on tropical rain forests is pumped right back into the atmosphere by the trees (see p. 45).

SUPERCYCLE

The most long-term part of the water cycle involves water carried down into Earth's interior, along with ocean-floor rock. This happens when a plate of Earth's oceanic crust is pushed beneath a continental plate (see p. 17). After millions of years water may erupt from volcanoes as vapor and rejoin the water cycle.

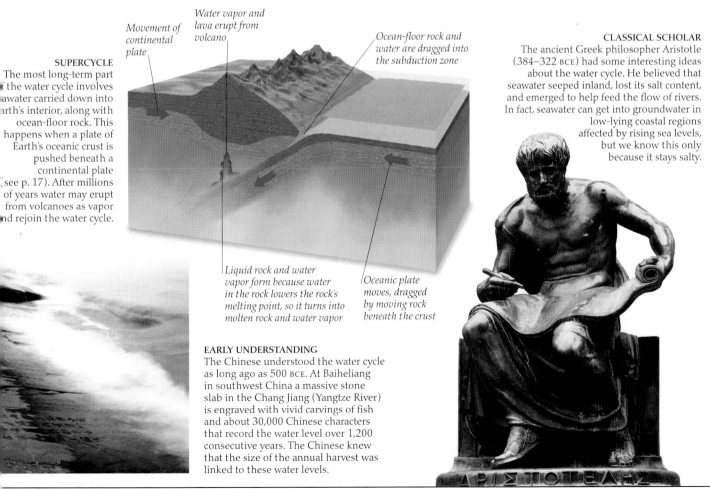

Movement of
continental
plate

Water vapor and
lava erupt from
volcano

Ocean-floor rock and
water are dragged into
the subduction zone

Liquid rock and water
vapor form because water
in the rock lowers the rock's
melting point, so it turns into
molten rock and water vapor

Oceanic plate
moves, dragged
by moving rock
beneath the crust

CLASSICAL SCHOLAR

The ancient Greek philosopher Aristotle (384–322 BCE) had some interesting ideas about the water cycle. He believed that seawater seeped inland, lost its salt content, and emerged to help feed the flow of rivers. In fact, seawater can get into groundwater in low-lying coastal regions affected by rising sea levels, but we know this only because it stays salty.

EARLY UNDERSTANDING

The Chinese understood the water cycle as long ago as 500 BCE. At Baiheliang in southwest China a massive stone slab in the Chang Jiang (Yangtze River) is engraved with vivid carvings of fish and about 30,000 Chinese characters that record the water level over 1,200 consecutive years. The Chinese knew that the size of the annual harvest was linked to these water levels.

Convection cell

Wind blowing north swerves east

Air cools in upper atmosphere

Sinking dry air creates subtropical deserts

Tropical rain clouds

Earth spins counterclockwise toward the east

Low-level winds meet at the Inter-Tropical Convergence Zone

GLOBAL AIR CURRENTS
The Sun warms the planet's surface, heating the air in the lower atmosphere so that it rises, flows sideways, cools, and sinks in loops called convection cells. These cells transport heat and water vapor, and create low-level winds. Because of the Earth's spin, these winds swerve toward the west or east to carry moist oceanic air and rainfall over the continents.

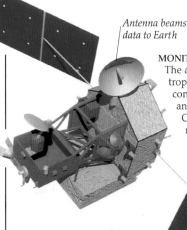

TROPICAL RAINS
Air currents rise in the tropics near the equator, flow north and south at high altitude, sink in the subtropics, then flow back toward the equator at low level, and meet again. The warm, moist, tropical air rises and builds up storm clouds, seen as a distinct band in this satellite image. The clouds spill torrential rain, creating rain forests where it falls on land.

Antenna beams data to Earth

MONITORING TROPICAL RAINS
The area at the equator where the low-level tropical winds from the north and south converge (meet) to form rising air currents and tropical rain is called the Inter-Tropical Convergence Zone (ITCZ). It is constantly monitored from space by craft such as the Tropical Rainfall Measuring Mission (TRMM) satellite—the first space mission dedicated to measuring tropical and subtropical rainfall.

Solar panels provide power for the satellite

Water and climate

THE CLIMATES OF THE WORLD are created by the heat of the Sun or lack of it, the position and size of the continents, and the changing weather, which is driven by solar power and the energy stored in water vapor. The climate helps define the character of a landscape—whether it is green and lush, barren and dusty, or buried beneath ice and snow. Where there is plenty of liquid water, plants can flourish and support a lot of animals. But where the water has either evaporated or frozen, life is either put on hold or cannot survive. The water-fueled weather machine even affects the ocean and its ability to support marine life.

SUBTROPICAL DESERT
As air flows away from the rain-forest zone at high altitude, it loses all its water vapor. The dry air sinks over the subtropics to the north and south, heats up, and absorbs any moisture from the ground to create arid deserts with very little vegetation like the Sahara, seen here, and the barren heart of Australia.

RAIN SHADOWS
Oceanic weather carries rain from the sea over the land, but if it runs into high mountains, they catch most of the rain. When the air gets beyond the mountains it is much drier, so the land is not as lush and green, and is in what is called a rain shadow. The rain shadow effect can be seen in this satellite image of the Himalayas, where most of the rain falls south of the mountain ridge.

WILLIAM FERREL
The 19th-century American meteorologist William Ferrel showed how some of the air that sinks over the subtropics flows toward the poles, swerving east. These warm winds run into polar air, generating cyclones that sweep east off the oceans and bring rain to northern Europe and northwestern America.

MONSOON SEASON
Since big continents are much colder than oceans in winter, they cool the air and make it sink. In Asia this makes dry air flow south over India, causing months of drought. But in summer the continent warms up, warming the air so it rises and draws moist air in from the ocean. The wind changes direction in a seasonal shift called a monsoon, and the drought is replaced by torrential rain. Monsoon rains are the only source of water for 70 percent of the crops in India, so many people celebrate the arrival of the rains.

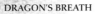

OCEANS AND CONTINENTS
Since water takes a long time to warm up and cool down, oceans never get as cold or as warm as continents. The climates of regions that lie close to big oceans are influenced by this, so they have mild winters and cool summers. This ice-covered house in British Columbia, Canada, is far from the ocean, in an area where winters are colder, and summers are much hotter.

DRAGON'S BREATH
The summer monsoon rains are vital to agriculture over most of southern Asia. For the Chinese, the rains were symbolized by the dragon, a creature of the heavens and of the rivers. At times they could be violent—just like the fire-breathing dragon—but they were also the bearers of the precious, essential gift of water.

27

Drought and flood

WATER IS BOTH A VITAL RESOURCE and a destructive force. When unusual weather brings too little rain, crops wither, farm animals can die, and people may starve. When there is too much rain, flash floods can leave trails of destruction, and rising rivers can overflow their banks and swamp whole landscapes. The floodwater can make sewers overflow and contaminate drinking water supplies, wreck power plants and leave people without electricity, and destroy homes and transportation links. Both extremes of drought and flood have been part of human experience for centuries, but as climates change and populations grow, droughts and floods seem to be becoming more frequent, and are having more devastating impacts.

HEAT AND DUST
If heat causes the moisture in the ground to evaporate faster than it is replaced by rainfall, over a long period, this causes a drought. As groundwater levels fall, shallow-rooted crops and grasses wither and die. Farm animals run out of both food and water, and may die, too—like these cattle in Kenya in 2006. In extreme cases whole landscapes can turn to desert, causing famine and mass migrations of people.

RISING WATERS
The heat that causes droughts also makes ocean water evaporate and form huge rainclouds, so while some areas may suffer years of drought, others are deluged with rain. Rivers burst their banks, and as the groundwater level rises the landscape is submerged. The flood that swamped the German city of Dresden was one of many caused by record rainfall in 2002.

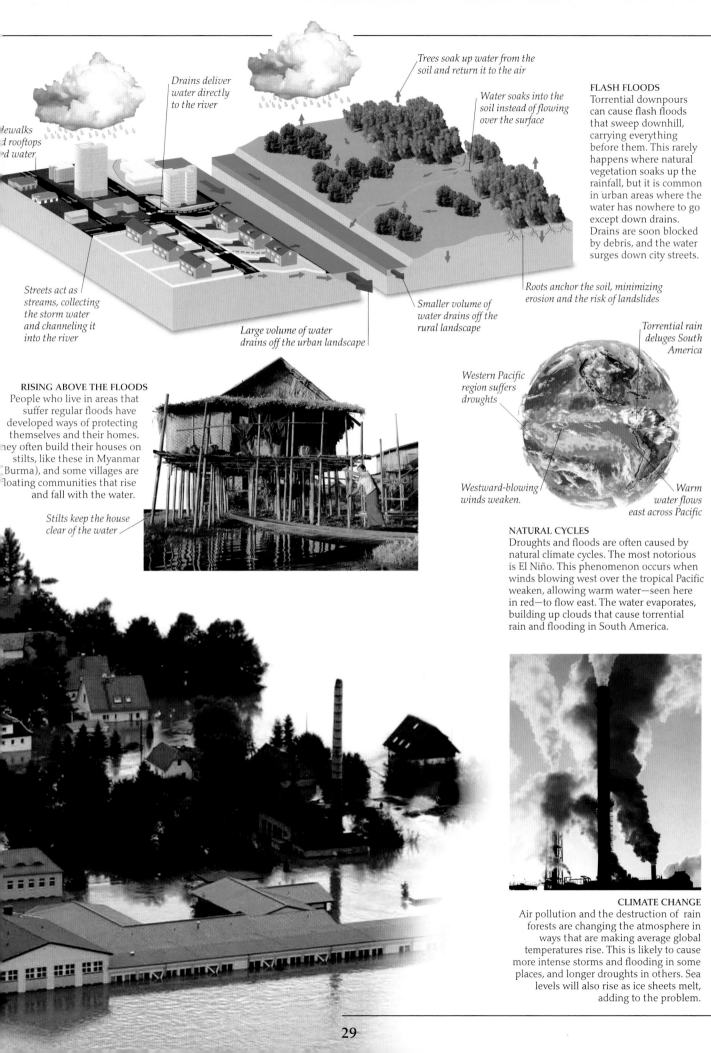

Drains deliver water directly to the river

Trees soak up water from the soil and return it to the air

Water soaks into the soil instead of flowing over the surface

ewalks
rooftops
water

Streets act as streams, collecting the storm water and channeling it into the river

Large volume of water drains off the urban landscape

Smaller volume of water drains off the rural landscape

Roots anchor the soil, minimizing erosion and the risk of landslides

FLASH FLOODS
Torrential downpours can cause flash floods that sweep downhill, carrying everything before them. This rarely happens where natural vegetation soaks up the rainfall, but it is common in urban areas where the water has nowhere to go except down drains. Drains are soon blocked by debris, and the water surges down city streets.

RISING ABOVE THE FLOODS
People who live in areas that suffer regular floods have developed ways of protecting themselves and their homes. They often build their houses on stilts, like these in Myanmar (Burma), and some villages are floating communities that rise and fall with the water.

Stilts keep the house clear of the water

Torrential rain deluges South America

Western Pacific region suffers droughts

Westward-blowing winds weaken.

Warm water flows east across Pacific

NATURAL CYCLES
Droughts and floods are often caused by natural climate cycles. The most notorious is El Niño. This phenomenon occurs when winds blowing west over the tropical Pacific weaken, allowing warm water—seen here in red—to flow east. The water evaporates, building up clouds that cause torrential rain and flooding in South America.

CLIMATE CHANGE
Air pollution and the destruction of rain forests are changing the atmosphere in ways that are making average global temperatures rise. This is likely to cause more intense storms and flooding in some places, and longer droughts in others. Sea levels will also rise as ice sheets melt, adding to the problem.

Erosion and weathering

THE LAND GRADUALLY wears away and water plays a key role in this. Water breaks down rock into smaller particles as it freezes and thaws, as well as by chemical reactions that dissolve the minerals holding rocks together. These are weathering processes. If water transports the particles and dissolved minerals from one place to another, the process is known as erosion. The particles and dissolved minerals are carried downhill to the oceans. Here the particles form seafloor sediments that are eventually compressed into sedimentary rocks. The minerals are recycled by marine life, which may also contribute to the formation of new rocks.

RELENTLESS GRIND
The more exposed a rock is, the more vigorously it is attacked. Softer rocks like sandstone are eroded faster than hard ones like granite, but this leaves the hard rocks more exposed and eventually they are ground away, too. As water or ice flowing off the land carries the rock debris away it carves deep valleys, gorges, and canyons.

Antelope Canyon, Arizona, eroded over thousands of years by torrents of sandy water during desert storms

DUMPING THE LOAD
Rock debris is swept away by rivers and glaciers. Rivers abandon heavy rocks when they slow down, followed by smaller stones, sand, and finally very small mud particles. By contrast, moving ice may carry boulders and fine particles as far as it flows, dumping them on when the ice melts away. Boulders dumped by ice are known as glacial erratics. This erratic in Yorkshire, U.K., was dropped here about 13,000 years ago

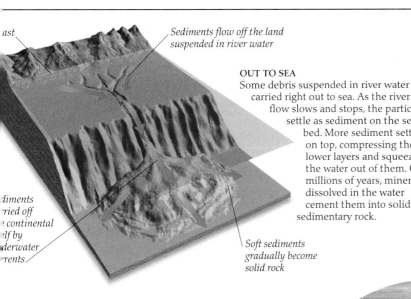

ast

Sediments flow off the land suspended in river water

OUT TO SEA
Some debris suspended in river water is carried right out to sea. As the river flow slows and stops, the particles settle as sediment on the sea bed. More sediment settles on top, compressing the lower layers and squeezing the water out of them. Over millions of years, minerals dissolved in the water cement them into solid sedimentary rock.

diments
ried off
e continental
elf by
derwater
rrents

Soft sediments gradually become solid rock

Granite   China clay

ROCK DECAY
Rainwater is slightly acid, and weathers rocks by dissolving some of their minerals. It even attacks hard granite by gradually breaking down its mica and feldspar crystals to form iron oxide, carbonate salts, and clays such as china clay. All that is left are tough quartz crystals, which survive as sand.

nestone
solved
dripping
ter forms
lactites

Stream plunges into sinkhole

Limestone pavement forms on surface as water seeps down through cracks

lagmite
ws up
m the
e floor

Burren limestone pavement, Ireland

Rock dissolves to create huge caverns

derground
am flows
ards sea

SOLUBLE LIMESTONE
Limestone is pushed up to the surface by earth movements. It forms dramatic landscapes, because it is easily dissolved by rainwater. Exposed rock on the surface forms fissured limestone pavements, and deep cracks are enlarged into complex cave systems. Underground streams carry the dissolved minerals away to the oceans, where they are recycled by marine life.

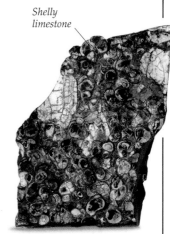

Shelly limestone

CARBONATE RECYCLING
The weathering of many rocks, including granite and limestone, produces dissolved minerals called carbonates. These are carried into the sea where marine organisms use them to build their shells and skeletons. When they die, their remains settle on the seabed, and build up in layers that are compressed to form carbonate rocks such as limestone, which often contains visible shell fragments.

ANCIENT REEF
The Yucatán Peninsula in Mexico was once a vast underwater reef created by corals that used dissolved carbonates to make limestone. Raised above sea level and exposed to tropical rain, the limestone has been undermined over thousands of years by underground streams fed by sinkholes called cenotes. These were vital water sources for the ancient Mayan civilization.

Streams and rivers

AS WATER DRAINS OFF THE LAND it creates a network of streams and rivers. These carve deep valleys through the uplands and carr off the rocky debris to the lowlands. Over time, this changes the whole shape of the land. They also transport the plant nutrients that help make the lowlands fertile, so they are vital to farming and civilization. The lower reaches of rivers are important transportation routes, but they also act as barriers to overland movement. So river ports and bridges have always been commercially and strategically important, attracting settlements that have grown into towns and cities.

TRICKLES AND SPRINGS
Rainwater draining downhill forms trickles and rivulets, which link up to form streams that cut shallow channels. In places water that has soaked into the ground meets a layer of impermeable (waterproof) rock and emerges as a freshwater spring. Many great rivers can be traced back to springs of this kind, which are sometimes named as the river source.

SCULPTING THE LAND
As streams flow downhill from upland ridges, particles of sediment suspended in the water scour the rock to carve valleys in the hillsides. This is one of the most powerful forms of erosion, grinding down mountains and creating valley networks that look like the twigs and branches of trees. Each branching valley network forms a drainage basin.

FERTILE PLAINS
Heavy rain or melting snow can swell lowland rivers so they flood the surrounding landscape. Since the floodwater stops flowing, it drops all the small particles it is carrying, and when the flood recedes it leaves a layer of fine sediment. Over the centuries this develops into very fertile soil. If flooding is controlled, floodplains make excellent farmland.

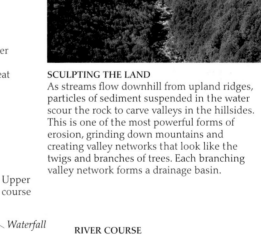

Upper course

Waterfall

Middle course

RIVER COURSE
An upland river is fast-flowing, with waterfalls and deep gorges. When it gets to flatter ground it slows down and drops some of the sediment it eroded from the uplands to form a broad floodplain. It often winds across its floodplain in a series of looping meanders. Eventually it dumps the last of its sediment in a muddy tidal estuary or extended delta as it flows into the sea.

Floodplain floods when the river overflows its banks

Oxbow lake forms when a meander is cut off from the river by erosion

Lower course

Meander is a looping bend

Delta is a huge fan-shaped area of sediment deposits

RIVER MANAGEMENT

Since floodplains make such good farmland and are often the sites of riverside towns, efforts are made to control flooding. These include raised banks and barrages that control the flow of water downstream. Tidal rivers can also flood because of very high sea levels. In the UK, the Thames Barrier (left) protects London from unusually high tides.

RIVER TRANSPORTATION

Rivers were once important transportation routes, with riverboats such as this Mississippi steamer carrying thousands of passengers each week. Faster road and rail transportation has now become far more important, but rivers can still provide a very economic, if slow way of moving heavy freight.

Funnel for smoke from the steam engine

Stern paddle-wheel propels the boat forward

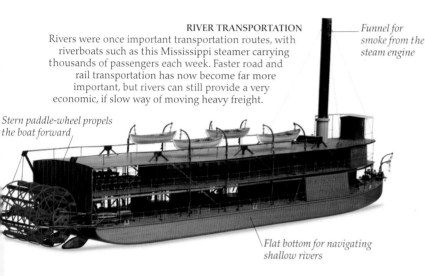

Flat bottom for navigating shallow rivers

RIVER ON MARS

Branching valleys on Mars show that big rivers once flowed across its surface. This image shows one of these valleys, with a fan of sediment spilling out over lower land. The valleys are now dry and most of the water on the planet appears to be frozen, but it is possible that there is liquid water beneath the surface.

STRATEGIC CROSSING

Bridges over major rivers have always been important focal points for commerce, because so many people use them. Invading armies would also converge on these crossings, so they were heavily defended and often destroyed. This was the fate of the stone bridge at Mostar in Bosnia, which was blown up during the Bosnian war in 1993. It has since been rebuilt.

Lakes and swamps

Fresh water does not always keep flowing toward the sea in streams and rivers. It can collect in ponds and lakes, or form wetlands such as peat bogs and swamps, which are also called marshes. Their nature varies according to climate, geology, and the plants and animals that live in them. They range from the cold, mosquito-infested peat bogs of northern mountains and Arctic tundra to the hot soda lakes of the African Rift Valley, with their spectacular flocks of flamingos. Some lakes are like freshwater seas, so broad that they extend way beyond the horizon. By contrast, many pools and wetlands are temporary, flooding only after heavy rain and drying up again within a few weeks.

STILL WATER
Upland lakes like Lake Tahoe in the United States have cold, pure water with few of the dissolved nutrients that support aquatic life, so they are often crystal clear. By contrast, many lowland lakes are much warmer and richer in nutrients, so they contain a lot of plankton, which makes the water cloudy.

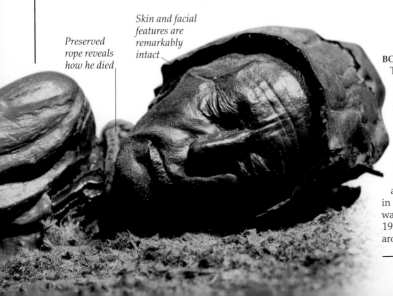

WILDLIFE HABITATS
Lakes and swamps are important habitats for wildlife such as this reed warbler, which nests in reedbeds and feeds its young on the teeming insects that hatch from the water. Over the years many wetlands have been drained and turned into rich farmland, but many others are now protected wildlife reserves.

EVOLVING WETLANDS
Fine mud settles among aquatic plants fringing lowland lakes, making the water shallower. Grassy plants colonize the shallow water, turning the lake into a swamp. Eventually water-tolerant woody plants such as these swamp cypresses take root in the mud, creating a wet woodland. Wet woodlands that receive heavy rain may be colonized by sphagnum moss that builds up in layers to create a peat bog.

Preserved rope reveals how he died

Skin and facial features are remarkably intact

BOG BURIAL
The waterlogged conditions in peat bogs and swamps prevent the activity of microbes that make things decay, so these wetlands can preserve wood and other materials. Some bogs in Scandinavia even preserve the remains of sacrificial victims such as Tollund Man, who died in the 4th century BCE. He was found in Denmark in 1950 with a rope still tied around his neck.

PEAT BOGS
Spongy plants called sphagnum mosses often spread over cold wetlands. As old moss dies the waterlogged conditions stop it from decaying, and its remains build up into a peat bog such the one that preserved Tollund Man.

SALT LAKES

In hot climates, water may form lakes that have no outlet because the water just evaporates. As it evaporates it leaves any dissolved salt behind. As more water flows in and evaporates, the salt content increases until the water is up to ten times as salty as the ocean. The Dead Sea in the Middle East is so salty that you can read a newspaper while floating in it.

Rock salt carved into a statue of the king and a miner

EVAPORITES

The salt that is left behind as salt lakes evaporate can build up in deep layers called evaporites. As the lake shrinks or even disappears the salt can be gathered and sold. Ancient evaporites have been found buried beneath later rocks, and are exploited by sinking salt mines. The salt in a Polish salt mine has been used to create this sculpture.

Mangrove tree with roots exposed at low tide

SALTMARSHES AND MANGROVES

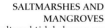

Sheltered tidal shores are often colonized by salt-tolerant plants. On cool coasts these form grassy or shrubby saltmarshes, but in tropical regions trees known as mangroves form dense, tidal swamp forests. The waterlogged mud is low in oxygen, so it is hostile to most plants, but the mangroves survive thanks to special roots that grow up like snorkel tubes to suck in vital oxygen.

INLAND SEA

Some lakes are so vast that they could easily be mistaken for inland seas. The five Great Lakes in North America—near the center of this satellite image—together form the largest continuous mass of fresh water on Earth, containing some 5,909 cubic miles (24,620 cubic km) of water.

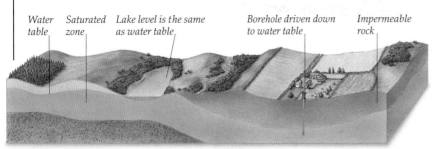

Water table | Saturated zone | Lake level is the same as water table | Borehole driven down to water table | Impermeable rock

Hidden water

A LOT OF RAINFALL SINKS into the ground, where it is soaked up by the soil. Some flows downhill and emerges to join streams. But some seeps straight down into permeable layers of rock, sand, or gravel that allow water to pass into and through them. This hidden groundwater is a precious resource, because it flows away toward the sea more slowly than surface water and only the groundwater closest to the surface evaporates into the air. So during dry seasons there are always reserves of water available, if you dig deep enough. There is even water deep below the surface in deserts, some of it thousands of years old.

THE WATER TABLE
Water draining down through soil, sand, and many rocks eventually reaches a layer of impermeable rock such as granite. This stops the water from sinking any farther, so the layers above it gradually become full, or saturated, with water. The upper limit of this saturated zone is called the water table.

PRECIOUS WATER
If you dig a hole that is deep enough to reach the water table, the bottom of the hole will fill with water to form a well. The water level in the well is that of the local water table. This 150-year-old well in Bhopal, India, proved a lifeline during a drought in 2003, when most other water sources in the city dried up.

Heathland forms on the infertile land

Minerals washed out of the upper layer

Some minerals form a dark layer

Deep layer contains minerals

SOILS AND DRAINAGE
Sandy or stony soil drains faster than fine-grained clay soil. As the water drains away it takes soluble alkaline minerals with it, making the upper layers acid and infertile. Only certain types of plants can cope with these conditions, often forming distinctive heathlands.

FLUCTUATING LEVELS
In wet seasons the water table can lie very near the ground surface, saturating the soil to create a swamp. During long droughts the water table can sink so far below the surface that even big lakes dry up. But the soil nearly always contains some water—especially if it has a lot of clay. Clay always consists of at least 17 percent water, however dry and cracked it looks.

AQUIFERS

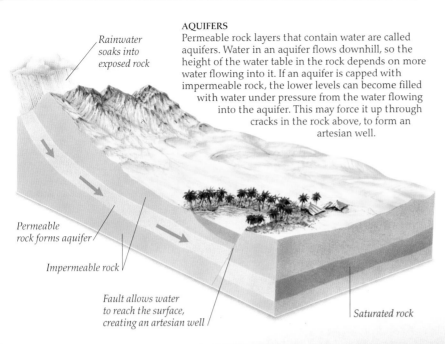

Permeable rock layers that contain water are called aquifers. Water in an aquifer flows downhill, so the height of the water table in the rock depends on more water flowing into it. If an aquifer is capped with impermeable rock, the lower levels can become filled with water under pressure from the water flowing into the aquifer. This may force it up through cracks in the rock above, to form an artesian well.

Rainwater soaks into exposed rock

Permeable rock forms aquifer

Impermeable rock

Fault allows water to reach the surface, creating an artesian well

Saturated rock

SPRINGS

If an impermeable rock layer emerges as an outcrop on a hillside, then any groundwater above it emerges too, at a spring. The water often flows from a row of springs tracing the top of the impermeable layer, and this is known as a spring line. The water is usually very clear because it has been filtered through the layers above the impermeable rock. If it contains minerals dissolved from the rocks, it is prized as mineral water.

FOSSIL WATER

[So]me natural underground water reservoirs were formed long ago [an]d capped by impermeable rock. Fossil water can escape to the [su]rface through a fault (above), or if wind erosion strips away the [roc]k on top. In the desert, this may create an oasis (below). The water [in] some oases is up to 20,000 years old. One of the biggest desert [re]servoirs lies beneath the eastern Sahara, with an estimated volume [of] 36,000 cubic miles (150,000 cubic km).

HYDROTHERMAL VEINS

Deep inside the Earth, water heated by contact with hot rock dissolves minerals. As the water flows away through cracks in the rock, it cools and the minerals crystallize in the cracks to form hydrothermal veins. Most of these veins consist of common minerals like quartz, but some contain precious metals, which are often mined.

MINERAL WATERS

Volcanically heated mineral water may emerge at the surface. It is often still warm, forming a thermal spring. Such mineral waters are believed to be good for the health. In the past, "taking the waters" was a popular therapy at spa towns such as Malvern in England, as seen here in 1855.

Frozen water

IN THE LOW TEMPERATURES of polar regions and on high mountains, most of the water in the environment is frozen into ice—either on land in the form of glaciers and ice sheets, or on the ocean as floating sea ice and icebergs. The landscape is also often thick with snow, which may survive in the cold climate for many years. The possibility that this polar and mountain ice might melt is one of the main risks associated with climate change, partly because meltwater flowing off continents into the oceans could cause catastrophic rises in sea level.

LOUIS AGASSIZ
In 1837 the Swiss zoologist Louis Agassiz put forward the idea that Earth experienced ice ages in the past. He came to this conclusion once he figured out that a lot of the landforms in northern Europe had been created by the erosive power of giant glaciers and the effects of frozen groundwater.

FROZEN SEAS AND LAKES
The ice on polar seas and winter lakes is formed by cold air freezing the surface of the water. On oceans the freezing process goes through various stages, including soupy grease ice, thin plates of pancake ice as seen here, and thick pack ice. On lakes and ponds where there is less water movement, the ice sheet is usually continuous.

Ice sheet flowing off Antarctica

Iceberg calving

Iceberg floats with most of its mass underwater, like all icebergs

GLACIERS AND ICE SHEETS
Glacier ice forms from snow that falls in such cold conditions that it does not melt. As more snow falls on top, its weight squeezes air out of the snowflakes and welds them into solid ice. The ice tends to creep downhill as glaciers, like this one flowing off an Arctic island and spilling into a frozen sea. In polar regions glacier ice can also form vast ice sheets such as those that cover Greenland and Antarctica. Where ice sheets extend over the sea, they are called ice shelves.

ICE CORES

Thick ice sheets build up in regions where the temperature is permanently below freezing, so the compacted snowflakes may be thousands of years old. The oldest ice found so far dates back to about 650,000 years ago. The ice contains pockets of air and particles of pollen and dust that were trapped when the ice first formed. Scientists extract columns, or cores, of ice from the ice sheets, and analyze the air and particles within to discover valuable information about past climates.

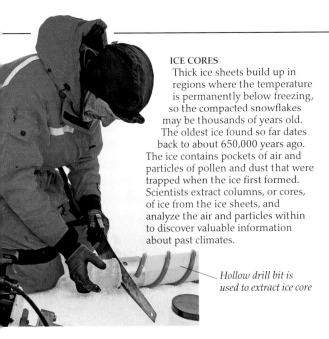

Hollow drill bit is used to extract ice core

PERMAFROST

In the Arctic tundra, water seeping into the ground freezes solid. It may thaw near the surface in summer, but the deeper levels stay frozen. This permafrost layer prevents water from draining away, so the summer meltwater forms vast tracts of swampland. The permafrost contains the deep-frozen remains of extinct animals such as this baby mammoth, whose 40,000-year-old remains were found in Siberia in 1977.

Skin preserved by the ice

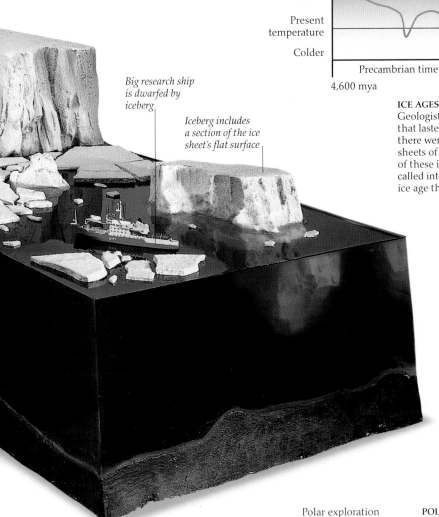

Big research ship is dwarfed by iceberg

Iceberg includes a section of the ice sheet's flat surface

Warmer				
Present temperature				
Colder				
Precambrian time	Palaeozoic Era	Mesozoic Era	Cenozoic Era	
4,600 mya	570 mya	225 mya	65 mya	2 mya

ICE AGES

Geologists divide Earth's long history into different time periods that lasted millions of years. During some of these time periods there were episodes when much of the planet was covered by vast sheets of ice and snow. These episodes are known as ice ages. Each of these ice ages had cold phases, called glacials, and warm phases called interglacials. We are now experiencing an interglacial in an ice age that started about 2 million years ago (mya).

ARCTIC OCEAN

Arctic Circle

ASIA   Bering Strait   **NORTH AMERICA**

Bering Sea

PACIFIC OCEAN

ICE AND SEA LEVEL

During the last ice age, so much water was locked up as ice that sea level fell by 300 ft (100 m). This turned shallow seas like the Bering Strait between Asia and North America into dry land (pale brown above). Sea level rose again when the ice melted. Further melting caused by global warming may make it rise even more.

ICEBERGS

When glaciers and ice sheets flow to the sea, chunks of [ic]e break off and float away as icebergs. So icebergs are [n]ot sea ice but glacier ice formed from compressed [s]now. They float with about 90 percent of their bulk [u]nderwater, so they are much bigger than they look. [S]ome of the icebergs that break off, or calve, from [A]ntarctic ice sheets are vast, floating ice islands that [m]ay drift for years before melting away into the ocean.

Polar exploration sled from the 1930s, loaded with supplies

POLAR EXPLORATIONS

Icebound landscapes are virtually lifeless, because most forms of life cannot function in places where all liquid water is turned to ice. Warm-blooded animals and people can survive, but only with difficulty. So polar exploration is dangerous, and many brave explorers have died there.

Water of life

ALL LIVING ORGANISMS DEPEND ON WATER. Most life-forms live in water, and all life forms on Earth are composed almost entirely of water. Many chemicals dissolve in water, allowing them to mix together and react to create the complex molecules of life. Water's ability to dissolve many substances also makes it an excellent medium for transporting dissolved chemicals, including nutrients, gas, and waste, into and out of living cells. All living organisms must retain a certain level of water to sustain normal life processes. If a living organism loses too much water, it dies. Water's unique life-giving properties mean it is likely that life itself began in water.

SINGLE CELL
The simplest life-forms are single-celled, microscopic packets of watery fluid like this desmid. Single-celled organisms use chemicals dissolved in water to make substances called proteins. The proteins make up part of the structure of the cell and enable it to grow and reproduce.

PHOTOSYNTHESIS
Plants use sunlight's energy to make their own food from air and water in a process called photosynthesis. Chlorophyll, a green chemical in the plant, absorbs the energy and uses it to split water into hydrogen and oxygen. The hydrogen is combined with carbon dioxide from the air to make sugar, an energy-rich food.

Mats of microscopic bacteria flourish in the hot, chemically rich water

PRODUCERS AND CONSUMERS
While some living things produce food, others—including all animals—consume it. They eat the food producers, or consume them secondhand by eating other consumers. They break down the carbohydrates, proteins, and other complex substances, and combine the ingredients with water to build new tissues.

Plant makes sugar and proteins that are eaten by the caterpillar for energy

Caterpillar's food is broken down by digestion so the animal can absorb sugar and other nutrients

LIFE BEGINS
Earth may have looked like this in its early history about 3.5 billion years ago. At this time cyanobacteria, some of the first photosynthetic organisms, began to build up column-shaped stromatolites in the seas, as seen here. The first life forms were even simpler than cyanobacteria, and probably appeared through chemical reactions in hot pools of water about 3.8 billion years ago.

Pond water under
the microscope

CRADLE OF LIFE
Most life is either oceanic or depends on
cool rainwater. But some bacteria—the
simplest living organisms—live in extreme
environments such as this hot spring in
Yellowstone National Park, where the acidified
water can be a scalding 175°F (80°C). These
bacteria are very similar to fossils of the earliest
known life forms, so it is likely that life
began in hot water like this.

LIVING WATER
Water is the main ingredient of all
living things, which could not
function without it. Water is also
the habitat where most of them live.
A single drop of pond water often
contains hundreds of microscopic
organisms, such as these euglenas,
desmids, and diatoms. Together they
form a tiny living world supported by
light, air, and water.

Living in water

SINCE WATER IS VITAL TO LIFE, it makes an ideal habitat for living organisms—especially simple ones that absorb dissolved nutrients and gases through their skins. But it is also a good environment for many other reasons. Liquid water is never very cold and only rarely very hot. It enables many animals to thrive without having to move around, because unlike air, it carries a lot of food that can be caught easily as it drifts by. It also supports the weight of animals, so they do not need strong skeletons. So it is no surprise that the greatest diversity of life flourishes in the world's oceans, lakes, and rivers.

AQUATIC PLANTS
Water is essential to plants, which use it to make food. Some plants, such as this water lily, are adapted to live either on or under the water of rivers and lakes, where they never risk drying out. Their specialized roots can take in oxygen from the water. All plants use oxygen to extract energy from their food.

MICROSCOPIC PLANKTON
The smallest aquatic organisms are bacteria and microscopic algae, such as these diatoms. They drift in sunlit water as plankton, and make food by photosynthesis, just like green plants. They are eaten by tiny animals that drift around with them, and both are eaten by larger plankton-eaters such as freshwater insects and fish. So plankton support all other aquatic animals.

CRAWLERS AND GRAZERS
Many aquatic animals such as snails, crabs, starfish, and this amazingly well-camouflaged sea slug live by crawling about on the seabed, or over seaweeds and coral reefs. They graze on algae or rooted animals that cannot escape, or they scavenge the remains of marine animals.

ROOTED TO THE SPOT
Many aquatic animals such as this sea anemone cling to rocks and let the water bring them a steady supply of food. A lot of these animals live as plankton when they are young, drifting in the water and settling only when they turn into adults.

LIVING REEF
Clear tropical seas contain very little plankton (see p. 18), so tropical corals must add to their food supply by teaming up with microscopic organisms, or microbes. The microbes live inside the coral and make sugar from water and oxygen. They pass some sugar to the coral in exchange for protein-building nutrients. The sugar gives corals the energy to build coral reefs.

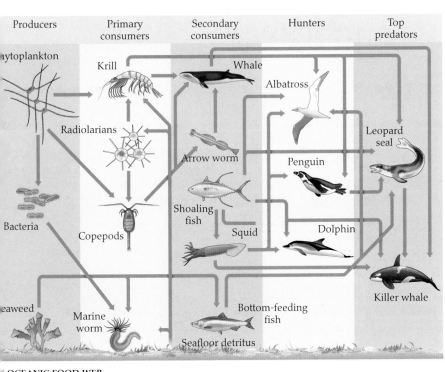

Producers	Primary consumers	Secondary consumers	Hunters	Top predators

Phytoplankton

Krill

Whale

Albatross

Leopard seal

Radiolarians

Arrow worm

Penguin

Bacteria

Shoaling fish

Copepods

Squid

Dolphin

Seaweed

Marine worm

Bottom-feeding fish

Seafloor detritus

Killer whale

OCEANIC FOOD WEB

[In] the ocean, producers are eaten by primary consumers such as copepods. [Th]ese are eaten by secondary consumers such as squid, which are hunted by [an]imals such as dolphins. Dolphins may fall prey to top predators such as [kil]ler whales. However, life is more complicated than this, because most [an]imals also eat creatures at other levels in the system. So instead of being [pa]rt of a simple food chain, oceanic animals interact in a complex food web.

THE WRONG TYPE OF WATER

Most aquatic animals live either in fresh water or in salty seas. If they enter the wrong type of water, their body fluids gain or lose water until their salt content matches that of the environment. They swell up or dry out, and die. But some fish, such as these salmon, have adapted to avoid this when they migrate upriver from the sea to breed.

Feathery gills gather oxygen

BREATHING IN WATER

Most aquatic animals get the oxygen they need to breathe from the water instead of the air. Like this baby newt, they have feathery, thin-walled gills in place of lungs. As water passes over the gills, gases are exchanged. Oxygen seeps into the blood from the water, and carbon dioxide seeps out from the blood into the water. Some aquatic animals, such as corals and jellyfish, do not have gills, because the gases can pass through their thin skins instead.

STREAMLINED SWIMMERS

Water supports animals physically as well as providing them with food and oxygen. It is almost as dense as their bodies, so they can float above the ocean floor without using a lot of energy. But the density of water also makes moving through it difficult, so excellent streamlining is essential for animals that want to move fast. High-speed hunters such as this blue shark can swim at 25 mph (40 kph) or more.

Roots and leaves

THE FIRST ORGANISMS TO LIVE ON LAND were microscopic bacteria, algae, and fungi, which lived in permanently wet places where they were surrounded by water. Eventually, simple plants such as mosses evolved the ability to absorb and store water, but they were still confined to damp habitats, and could not grow very high above the source of their moisture. The evolution of plants with veins for pumping water through their roots, stems, and branches solved this problem, enabling the growth of tall trees. As plants developed more effective ways of surviving drought they were able to colonize most of the land.

Pseudomonas bacteria

TOUGH MICROBES
Microscopic single-celled bacteria like these can function only if they are wet, so on land they need to live in damp places. However, some of these microbes are able to survive drying out. They lie dormant (inactive), sometimes for several months, then revive and start multiplying when they get wet again.

Thalloid liverwort

GREEN CUSHIONS
Mosses and liverworts were the first green plants to appear on land about 470 million years ago. Most mosses and liverworts are low-growing plants that absorb water over their whole surface, often forming compact spongy cushions that store water after rainfall. They can survive dry periods, but they need water to grow and reproduce.

Open cap shrivels up after scattering spores

FUNGI
Fungi are utterly different from plants. They cannot make their own food, so they absorb food made by other organisms. They need a lot of water, forming extensive root networks that soak up water from soil or waterlogged timber. The mushrooms that appear on the surface are temporary reproductive structures that scatter their spores.

Closed cap holds spores

Fly agaric mushrooms

Yellow lichen can grow on bare rock

Soil conceals extensive root system

LICHENS
Fungi are very good at soaking up rainwater and dissolved minerals. Some form partnerships with microscopic algae that are able to make food by photosynthesis, like plants, but need a reliable water supply. These partnerships are called lichens. They can live almost anywhere, including bare rock, lying dormant during dry periods and growing slowly when they are wet.

Fern frond contains vein network

PIPED WATER
Around 400 million years ago, ferns evolved the vein networks that carry water up their stems to their leaves, where it is used to make sugar. The veins, shown here in the cross-section illustration, allowed ferns to grow well above the ground on tall stems, and evolve into some of the first trees 300 million years ago.

Cortex helps support the stem

Bundles of veins carry water or sugary sap

Bracken fern

Section through fern stem

FOSSIL FUEL
Over 200 million years ago, forests of tree ferns grew on swampy land. When the trees died and fell into the swamp, the watery conditions stopped them from decaying. The dead ferns formed deep layers of peat, which over millions of years became coal. Coal from mines such as this one powered the steam engines of the industrial revolution in the 18th and 19th centuries. Today, most electricity plants are powered by coal.

WATER PUMP
Trees rely on vein networks that are very like those of ferns. They work by a process called transpiration. As the Sun warms the tree, water in its leaves turns to water vapor that enters the atmosphere. That is why trees play a key role in the water cycle (see pp. 24–25). The evaporated water is replaced by more water drawn from the twigs, branches, trunk, and roots. The system pumps water to the top of the tree, which in this American redwood may be 300 ft (100 m) above the ground.

Dried-up resurrection plant

Revived resurrection plant

SURVIVING DROUGHT
Water is vital to plants, but many are able to survive long periods of drought. Some, such as prickly cacti and similar succulent plants, store water in their stems and leaves. Other drought-resistant plants can dry out and miraculously revive when they get wet again. The "resurrection plant" of the American deserts is a type of moss that can survive for months like this.

Living on dry land

ANIMALS STARTED LIVING ON LAND about 420 million years ago. They were creatures like modern woodlice, which could lose moisture from their bodies easily because they did not have waterproof skins. This meant they were restricted to damp places where their bodies could absorb the moisture they needed to function properly. When the first land-dwelling vertebrates (animals with backbones) joined them they suffered the same problem. Most of these animals also had to breed in water, as most frogs still do. But over time animals such as insects and reptiles developed waterproof skins and ways of breeding on dry land.

WATER TO LAND
The first land animals were basically aquatic animals that were able to absorb oxygen from the air through their moist skins. To do this—and to keep from drying out—they had to live in wet places. Many soil animals such as these earthworms still live in the same way.

KEEPING THE MOISTURE IN
The first reptiles evolved from amphibians (see left) about 340 million years ago. Reptiles can live in habitats that would be unsuitable for water-dependent amphibians because, unlike amphibians, reptiles have scaly waterproof skin and waterproof eggs. A reptile's skin keeps in essential moisture that the animal's body needs to function properly. As seen here, the egg keeps in fluid that keeps the unborn reptile moist, so the eggs do not need to be laid in water.

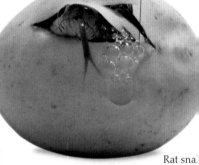

Fluid from inside the egg

Rat snake hatching from its egg

WET AND DRY
Amphibians evolved from fish and became the first vertebrates to live on land about 400 million years ago. Although amphibians can breathe air and live on land, they return to the water to mate. Many amphibian females lay their eggs in the water, then the male swims over them and fertilizes them with his sperm. Amphibians rely on water to keep the newly hatched young from drying out and dying. This strawberry poison dart frog has placed her tadpole in water in a bromeliad plant to keep the hatchling moist. Amphibians do not drink water but soak up as much as they need through their thin skin.

DRINKING
Aquatic animals get all the water their bodies need to function in their food, or absorb it through their skins. Some small land animals can live in the same way, but others must find water to drink. In hot, dry climates such as the African savanna grasslands, animals lose moisture easily and water is scarce. Large animals like these zebras may travel long distances every day to drink from scattered waterholes, otherwise they would not have enough water in their bodies for the life processes that keep the animals alive.

SURVIVING DROUGHT
Unlike plants, animals are able to avoid droughts by moving to areas where the grass is still green. Some animals spend most of their lives on the move, such as these wildebeest crossing the dry African plains. Other animals go to ground, such as the desert toads that stay buried in waterproof cocoons until it rains.

SHIPS OF THE DESERT
Camels can travel for days without water because they do not start to sweat (see p. 49) until their body temperature rises well above the normal 98.6°F (37°C). This ability was exploited by the traders of the Sahara and Central Asia, who used camels instead of packhorses to carry their goods. This illustration from a medieval map shows the camel train of explorer Marco Polo on the Silk Road to China in the 13th century.

DESPERATE MEASURES
Most small desert animals stay in burrows all day to avoid the hot sun, and emerge at night when they are less likely to lose moisture. In the Namib Desert of southwest Africa, beetles wait for water vapor in the cool evening air to condense on their bodies as dew. They then lift their tails so the dew drips forward into their mouths.

Dew drops are pure water

Sensitive antennae can detect the scent of water

Long wings provide mobility

INSECT SWARMS
Many desert insects have short, fast lifecycles that are triggered by rare rainstorms. They hatch, feed, mate, and lay eggs in a few weeks while the desert is still green, and their eggs then lie dormant until the next storm. Locusts live like this, sometimes forming vast swarms that contain up to 50 billion insects. If such a swarm descends on a farmer's field, the hungry locusts can destroy the entire crop within an hour

Water in your body

Water makes up at least half of our body weight and it is the main component of each cell in our body. Water is involved in every bodily function, and many of these functions rely on the body losing water at a steady rate. We must replace the water we lose by drinking and eating regularly to stay healthy. Losing even 10 percent of our body weight in water is enough to make us seriously ill. If we are deprived of water for too long, we can die of thirst.

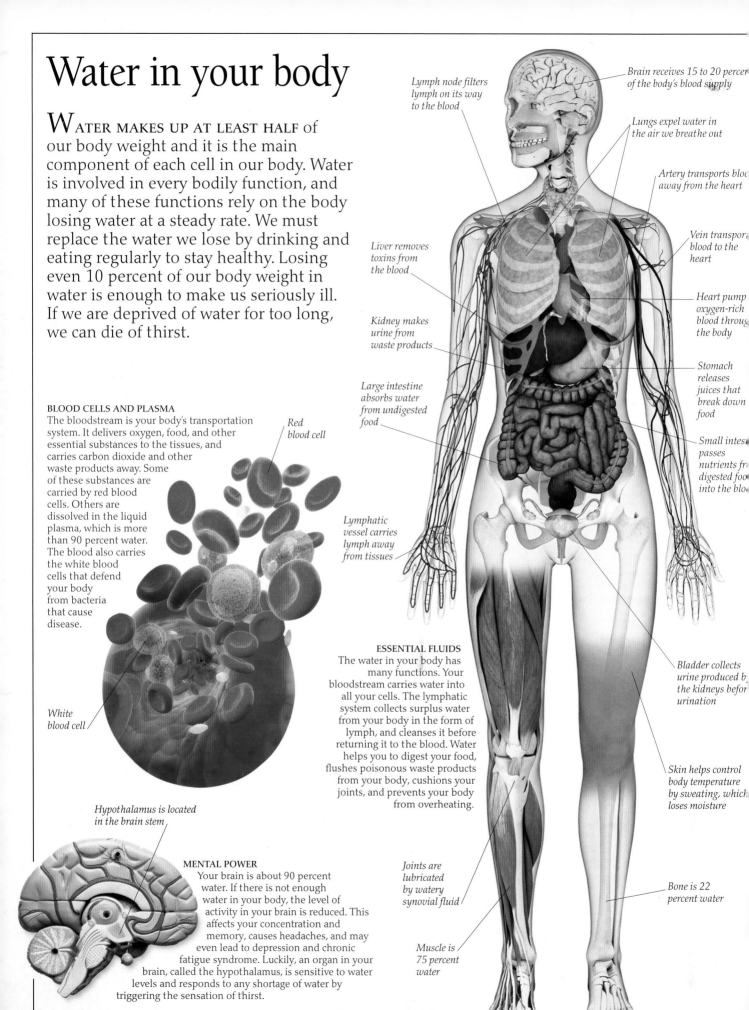

BLOOD CELLS AND PLASMA

The bloodstream is your body's transportation system. It delivers oxygen, food, and other essential substances to the tissues, and carries carbon dioxide and other waste products away. Some of these substances are carried by red blood cells. Others are dissolved in the liquid plasma, which is more than 90 percent water. The blood also carries the white blood cells that defend your body from bacteria that cause disease.

Red blood cell

White blood cell

Hypothalamus is located in the brain stem

MENTAL POWER

Your brain is about 90 percent water. If there is not enough water in your body, the level of activity in your brain is reduced. This affects your concentration and memory, causes headaches, and may even lead to depression and chronic fatigue syndrome. Luckily, an organ in your brain, called the hypothalamus, is sensitive to water levels and responds to any shortage of water by triggering the sensation of thirst.

Lymph node filters lymph on its way to the blood

Liver removes toxins from the blood

Kidney makes urine from waste products

Large intestine absorbs water from undigested food

Lymphatic vessel carries lymph away from tissues

ESSENTIAL FLUIDS

The water in your body has many functions. Your bloodstream carries water into all your cells. The lymphatic system collects surplus water from your body in the form of lymph, and cleanses it before returning it to the blood. Water helps you to digest your food, flushes poisonous waste products from your body, cushions your joints, and prevents your body from overheating.

Joints are lubricated by watery synovial fluid

Muscle is 75 percent water

Brain receives 15 to 20 percent of the body's blood supply

Lungs expel water in the air we breathe out

Artery transports blood away from the heart

Vein transports blood to the heart

Heart pumps oxygen-rich blood through the body

Stomach releases juices that break down food

Small intestine passes nutrients from digested food into the blood

Bladder collects urine produced by the kidneys before urination

Skin helps control body temperature by sweating, which loses moisture

Bone is 22 percent water

DIGESTIVE JUICES

During a meal, pits in the stomach lining pour about one pint (half a liter) of digestive juice onto your food. Special proteins called enzymes in the digestive juice start breaking down the food into useful nutrients. Deep in your intestines, more digestive juices continue the process. Your body absorbs the nutrients through the intestinal wall, along with most of the water.

Magnified view of stomach lining

WORKING UP A SWEAT

When you get too hot on a warm day, or if exercise is making you overheat, sweat glands release moisture, called perspiration, onto your skin. The warmth on your skin makes the perspiration evaporate, and as it evaporates the water absorbs heat energy from your skin, making it cooler. But this does mean that you lose body moisture. If your body loses too much water you become dehydrated. Athletes must drink a lot of water to avoid dehydration.

WATER AND FAT

Although water accounts for more than 70 percent of most body tissues, fat is less than 25 percent water. So the more fat there is in your body, the smaller the percentage of water. On average, a woman's body has more fat than a man's, so her body contains a smaller proportion of water. Being dehydrated can also make you fat, because the body removes water from fat cells and this makes it harder for the fat to be turned into energy.

60%

50%

Adult man   Adult woman

Solid waste ¼ pint (0.1 liter)

Breath ¾ pint (0.4 liter)

Sweat 1 pint (0.5 liter)

Urine 3 pints (1.5 liters)

LOSING WATER

Your body is losing water all the time. The blood-cleaning function of your kidneys relies on water to carry waste products away in the form of urine. Keeping cool in warm weather relies on perspiration, which involves losing water. You also lose moisture every time you breathe out, because your breath contains water vapor. You can see this on cold days when it forms a visible mist of water droplets.

An adult's daily water loss

WATER SOURCES

Clearly the main source of water is water itself. But we also get water from many other sources. They include milk and the other fluids that we drink. Water forms part of many raw foods such as fruit and vegetables, and the juices that we can extract from them. Cooked food also contains water. An adult needs to consume 4 pints (2 liters) of fluids and a healthy diet of food each day to replace the 5 pints (2.5 liters) of water lost from the body during one day.

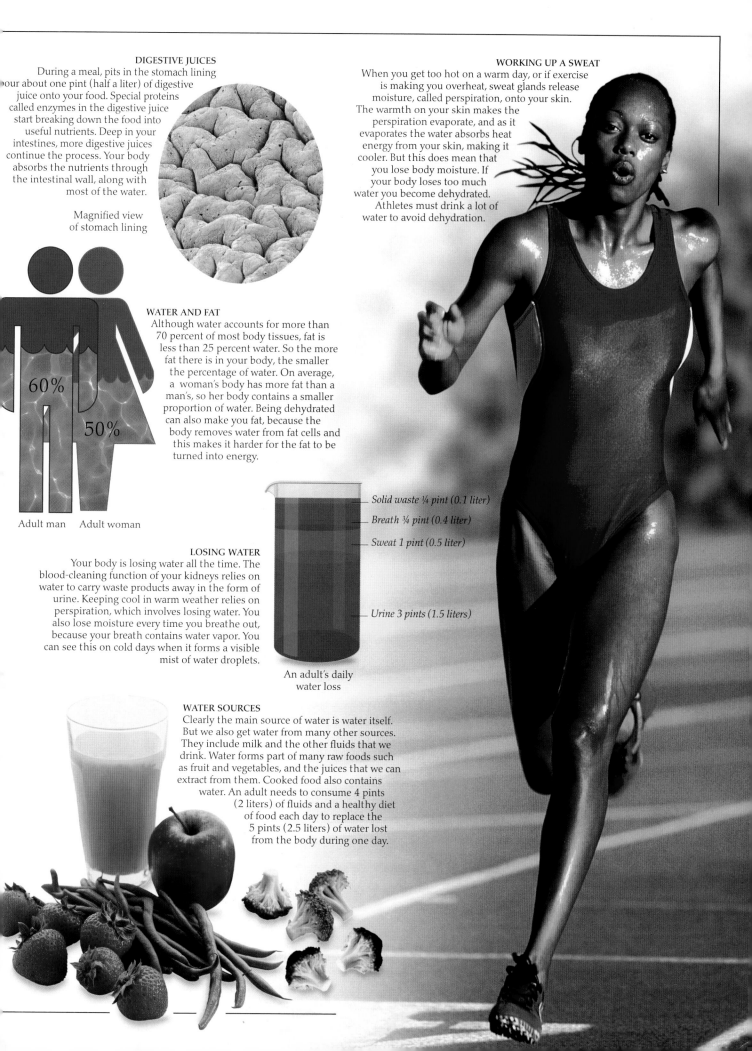

Water and health

ALTHOUGH WATER IS VITAL FOR SURVIVAL, it can also be a danger to health. This is because it can carry microbes that cause disease. Some of these are parasites that live inside their host's body and sap his or her strength. Others are bacteria called pathogens that cause deadly diseases. These microbes get into the water when sewage contaminates the water supply. For most of history people had no idea that microbes existed. Yet they did realize that techniques such as boiling made water safe to drink, and some of these processes are still part of daily life.

PRECIOUS RESOURCE

Clean, fresh water is the first and most vital requirement for health. In developed countries, where there are modern facilities and the income per person is relatively high, a reliable water supply is taken for granted. In many other parts of the world access to safe drinking water is a luxury. At least 884 million people still use sources of water that are likely to be contaminated with dangerous microbes. About 330 million of them live in Africa to the south of the Sahara. For these children in Zambia, southern Africa, the clean water flowing from this pump is a precious resource.

DIRTY WAT

About 80 percent of disease in developing countries caused by water contaminated with sewage. Wa contamination is a constant problem in shanty tow where poor people live in makeshift dwellings w no proper sanitation. It is also a major cause disease when wars or natural disasters wreck draina and water supply systems. These children in Baghd Iraq, may soon regret playing in this filthy wat

PARASITE ATTACK
Many people who live in places with poor water supplies suffer from intestinal parasites such as worms, flukes, or the microbe below, which can cause a serious illness called giardiasis. Tourists who visit these regions are also likely to pick up these dangerous parasites if they drink contaminated water, or even eat raw food that has been washed in such water.

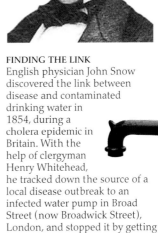

Microscopic parasite *Giardia*

FINDING THE LINK
English physician John Snow discovered the link between disease and contaminated drinking water in 1854, during a cholera epidemic in Britain. With the help of clergyman Henry Whitehead, he tracked down the source of a local disease outbreak to an infected water pump in Broad Street (now Broadwick Street), London, and stopped it by getting the pump handle removed.

The Broad Street pump

HEALTHY INFUSIONS
As long ago as 350 BCE the Greek physician Hippocrates recommended boiling drinking water to rid it of bad smells and tastes, which he associated with disease. Boiling the water did remove the smells and tastes. It also removed the harmful microbes that cause diseases, although Hippocrates had never heard of microbes. Neither had the eastern peoples who also discovered that boiling their water reduced the risk of infectious disease. They found that it tasted better if poured over tea leaves, and so invented the tradition of tea drinking.

Early 19th-century Japanese woodcut print of a tea-drinking ceremony

GRAPE AND GRAIN
Thousands of years ago, people in Europe discovered that wine or beer made from grapes or grain was safer to drink than water, because the alcohol killed any microbes, although this was not known at the time. But alcohol is poisonous to people, too, so the tradition had some unwelcome side-effects. These include diabetes, liver damage, heart disease, strokes, and throat cancer.

WATER TREATMENT
In most developed countries, the water supplied to homes is safe because it is filtered and treated with chlorine—the disinfectant that is also used in swimming pools. This destroys any bacteria and other organisms. Some people believe that chlorine may itself be a health hazard, but it is not nearly as dangerous as the pathogens it destroys.

WASH YOUR HANDS
Many health problems can be avoided by simply washing your hands frequently with hot water and soap. This is especially important before eating and after going to the bathroom, but also if you have any kind of illness such as a cold, because many infections are spread by physical contact. So although water can carry disease, it also provides one of the easiest ways of preventing it.

Water supply

Human health depends on a reliable supply of clean water. Long ago everyone dran the water from springs, rivers, and simple wells. But human populations are now so dense that the water from many of these sources is contaminated witl human waste, which can carry parasites and pathogens. A lot of people living in developing countries risk illness by drinking the water because they have no option. But in the developed world drinking water is treated to eliminate the disease organisms, and piped directl to houses and other buildings. Wastewater is piped into drainage systems that carry it to water treatment works to be made harmless.

RIVERS AND GLACIERS
Much of our water still comes from open sources such as streams and rivers, but it is generally treated to ensure it is safe to drink. Some countries use water that flows from glaciers, as seen here in the mountains of Chile. Glaciers act as natural reservoirs of clean water, but they are threatened by global warming.

DAMS AND RESERVOIRS
Water is stored in reservoirs. These can be created by building river dams such as the Hoover Dam in Colorado. Reservoirs ensure a reliable supply even in times of low rainfall. But they can fill up with river sediment that settles at the dam. Often when valleys are flooded to create reservoirs, villages and farmland are lost, and the river life is devastated.

WELLS AND BOREHOLES
These engineers in Zimbabwe are digging a traditional well—a deep hole that extends down to the water table (see p. 36). The water is collected with a bucket and windlass. Such wells are easily contaminated, but they can be made safer by sealing the well head and equipping it with a pump. The same principle is used to extract water from much deeper aquifers, using boreholes equipped with powered pumps.

Wooden
dousing rod

DOUSING

Some people locate
underground water by a
traditional technique called
water divining, or dousing. The
douser surveys a likely area by walking
slowly across it holding a forked stick or two
metal rods, though the equipment varies. If
carried across a hidden water source, the stick
or rods react by moving, apparently of their
own accord. It can work surprisingly well, but
no one knows why.

Desalinated water is piped
out of the filter and on to
the post-treatment facility

Saltwater flows through
membranes on its way
to the center of the
reverse osmosis filter

Intake valves
draw in salt
water from
the sea

Outlet releases
concentrated salt
water into
the sea

Power plant

Screen filters out
shells, wood, and
other debris

Control center

Storage tank

Desalinated
water is sent
off to be added
to the mains
water supply

Post-treatment facility
adds useful minerals
to the water

Reverse osmosis filtration
system removes the salt

Pipe carries concentrated
saltwater out to sea

DESALINATION

In hot countries with few fresh water resources, drinking water can be
made from seawater by removing the salt. The water is pumped through
banks of very fine filters at high pressure in a process called reverse
osmosis. The salt that is filtered out of the water is piped back to the sea.
The process uses a lot of energy, but it can be fueled by solar power.

Engineer uses
windlass to lower
inspector

SUPPLY PIPES AND SEWERS

Most people in the world have to use
a shared water supply, such as a village
well. But in all developed countries
water is delivered to individual homes
and workplaces through a system of
supply pipes. A similar network collects
wastewater from houses, feeding it into
big sewers like this that carry it to
wastewater treatment plants.

ANCIENT TECHNOLOGY

The ancient Romans built magnificent aqueducts such as the
Pont du Gard in southern France to supply water to cities.
These were linked to long channels running over the ground
or through tunnels. Engineers planned the course precisely
so that the water would flow at a steady rate downhill.

Household generates
wastewater

Wastewater is piped to
facility for treatment

Aeration of sludge
encourages the growth of
microorganisms that break
down organic matter

Bar screens
catch large
debris

Grit chamber allows
heavy particles to settle

Settling tank allows
smaller particles to
settle

Final treatment
removes harmful
nutrients

Clean water
released into river

Settling lagoon
permits waste
sludge removal

Trickling filter
converts dissolved
pollution into sludge

Truck removes
organic solids for
use as fertilizers

TREATING WASTEWATER

Wastewater is delivered through the sewers to a treatment plant. Here it is
filtered and passed through settlement tanks to remove most of the solids,
before being treated to destroy any harmful microbes. The treated water is
released in rivers or seas where it will be naturally purified long before
there is any chance that it will be extracted for use again.

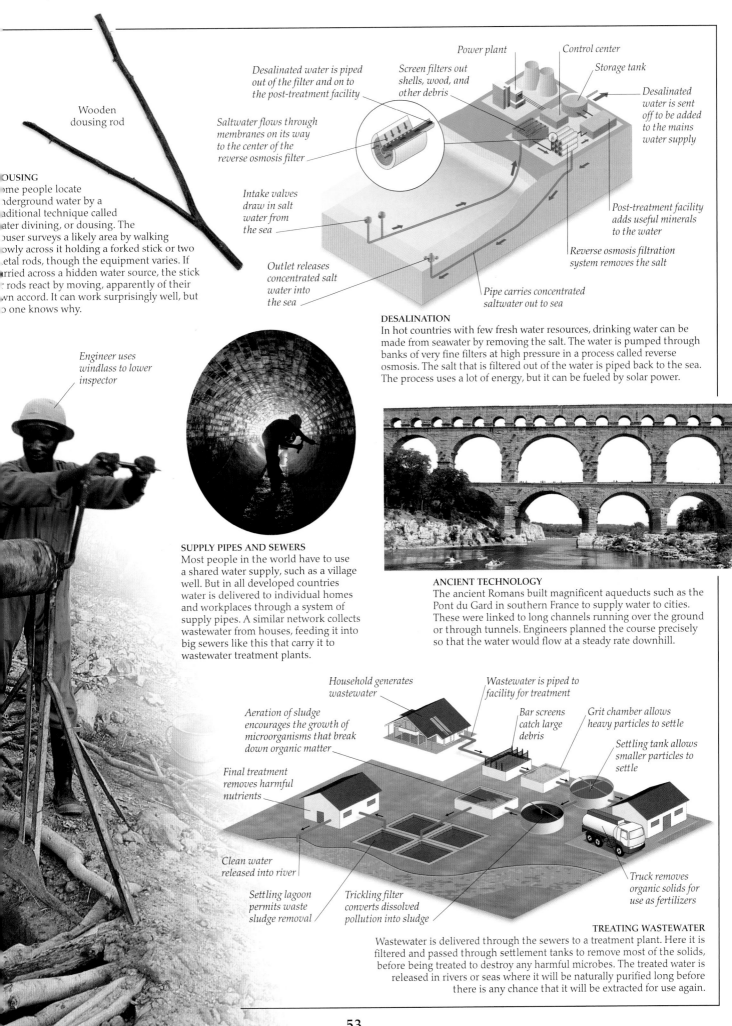

Farms and factories

W E USE HUGE QUANTITIES OF WATER IN THE HOME, but at eight percent of the total water used, domestic use is tiny when compared to the massive 69 percent used to keep farm animals and to irrigate, or artificially water, crops. Industrial processes, including mining and papermaking, use the remainder. Using water on a large scale can seriously reduce supplies, especially in times of low rainfall, and this can cause problems for other water users. Some forms of agriculture and industry also introduce pollutants into waste water that is deliberately or accidentally released into the environment.

ANCIENT IRRIGATION
In rice-growing regions that do not get daily tropical rain, paddy fields have to be irrigated—water is supplied to them artificially. In the past farmers used simple irrigation machines, such as the Archimedes screw in this 19th-century watercolor, to raise water from nearby rivers.

RICE FARMING
Rice grows best in paddy fields, which are like broad, but shallow pools. In the Asian tropics, where rice has been a staple food for centuries, rice paddies cover much of the farming landscape. In hilly areas, such as here in Guangxi Province, China, many of the hills have been carved into terraces with earth banks to retain the rainwater.

GREENING THE DESERT
Irrigation can be used to turn barren deserts into farmland. Water is piped to long sprinkler arms, which rotate to create circular patches of green, as here in Utah, US. But if the land is irrigated for too long, evaporation of the water adds so much salt to the soil that it becomes too infertile for farming.

Earthen bank allows the field to be flooded without water flowing away

FARM ANIMALS
It takes a lot of water to keep a farm animal. A dairy cow drinks more than 40 gal (150 liters) on a hot day. Even more water is used to clean that cow's milking equipment and housing, and for growing food for the animal.

HEAVY INDUSTRY
Water is used in huge quantities by industries such as papermaking—it took up to 2 pints (1 liter) of water to make this single sheet of paper. Metalworks such as this steel rod factory also use a lot of water for cooling both the product and the machines that make it. However, the water is not necessarily used up by these processes. It can be recycled in the factory or, if properly treated, returned to the environment.

HYDROPONICS
In some regions with little fertile farmland, crops are often grown under glass without soil. The system, known as hydroponics, uses just water containing dissolved nutrients, as seen in this glass jar. The method is often used in laboratories, and has even been proposed as a way of growing food in space.

Water carries away sand and stones to leave heavy gold

GOLD PANNING
During the US and Australian gold rushes of the 19th century, thousands of prospectors used water to separate gold from river sediments. Initially they would pan for gold by swirling sand and gravel in a pan of water. The heavier gold particles sank to the bottom of the pan and were separated out by gently swirling the lighter stony material over the rim.

Pools polluted with copper from a copper mine in Michigan

POLLUTION
Agriculture and industry can sometimes cause serious pollution of streams, rivers, and shallow seas. Fertilizer dissolved in water runs off agricultural land into bodies of water, which can become so fertile that certain algal species thrive. When they die the process of decay uses up the oxygen in the water, killing other wildlife. Toxic metals released by industry, such as lead and mercury, poison aquatic wildlife and make the water undrinkable. Some watercourses have even been known to contain radioactive waste.

Water nourishes the rice and prevents weeds from growing

Fishing and fish farming

Fishing has been a way of life for coastal, riverside, and lakeside communities for thousands of years. Some fish are caught by rod, or hand-thrown nets and traps in local waters. Far more fish are caught at sea by modern fishing vessels using the latest technology. Walls of nets and long lines of hooks, which are designed to catch fish in large numbers, often bring up by-catch, o species that are trapped unintentionally. Overfishing has reduced fish populations in many fishing grounds, so some seafood, such as salmon and shrimp, is now grown in fish farms to help meet demand.

RICH FISHERIES
Most of the richest fishing waters are shallow coastal seas where currents can scour nutrients from the seabed and bring them to the surface. Here they nourish swarms of plankton that feed big shoals of fish. The pale blue-green area in this satellite image of the Arctic is a plankton bloom.

SUSTAINABLE METHODS
For most of history fishing techniques were not efficient enough to have a serious impact on fish populations. Fish could breed fast enough to replace the numbers caught. Human populations were also much smaller. These lake fishermen in Burma (Myanmar) still use simple nets, watching for fish while paddling their boats with one oar. They do not catch more than they need and never run out of fish.

ANCIENT ART
Historical evidence of fishing, such as discarded fish bones and cave paintings, dates back 40,000 years. But people were probably fishing long before then. Many artists and authors have shown the importance of fishing to the people of their time in their work. This medieval painting illustrates a poem by the Greek author Oppian.

Reel releases and winds in fishing line

Trout rod (disassembled)

ROD AND LINE

For some people, fishing is just for fun. Most of these fishing enthusiasts fish with rods and lines and are known as anglers. They use bait and lures such as these imitation flies, which are designed to attract fish such as trout and salmon. Some anglers take away the fish for food, others return the fish alive to the water to sustain fish populations.

Hooks with fly lures

BIG BUSINESS

Sea fishing is now an industry, carried out by big boats such as these. They are equipped with electronic fish-finder equipment, great expanses of nets or immensely long multihooked longlines. They also have facilities for cleaning and freezing the catch on board. Often the boats must work in remote, stormy seas for months at a time because local fishing grounds have been overfished.

Conical net trap is dropped over freshwater carp, which is then speared

OVERFISHING AND BY-CATCH

Commercial fishing has become so efficient that many of the world's richest fishing grounds have been virtually fished out. At the same time many other species, such as albatrosses and sea turtles, are threatened with extinction because they are being trapped and drowned by fishing nets and hooks.

Young hawksbill turtle caught in a fishing net

Fishermen protesting against fishing controls, Scotland, UK

QUOTAS AND RESERVES

Governments control fisheries with quotas that limit the number of fish caught. The fish must also be big enough to have had a chance to breed and increase fish stocks. The measures are unpopular with fishermen, who are forced to throw back part of their catch. These British fishermen are protesting against the rules by dumping young fish on a city street.

FISH FARMING

These shrimp have been raised in coastal pools in the Far East, rather than caught from the wild. Such fish farming might seem an ideal solution to overfishing, but creating the pools damages coastal ecosystems, especially the mangroves that resist oceanic storms. Rearing fish in submerged, densely-stocked cages can pollute the water with excess fish food, droppings, parasites, and chemicals used to control disease. Also, some fish are fed on seafood caught in the wild.

Farmed shrimp

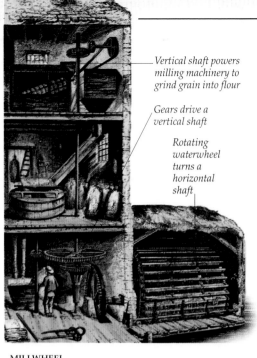

Vertical shaft powers milling machinery to grind grain into flour

Gears drive a vertical shaft

Rotating waterwheel turns a horizontal shaft

Water power

W ATER CAN BE TURNED INTO ENERGY in several ways, either directly through the power of flowing water, or indirectly by turning it into high-pressure steam. Steam can be used to drive engines—including the steam turbines that generate a lot of our electricity. Turning water into steam requires heat. This has to be produced by using other forms of energy such as burning fuel, so the water is just part of the process rather than the source of the energy. But flowing water has a power of its own, making burning fuel unnecessary, and modern techniques for harnessing this power can be efficient.

MILLWHEEL
Waterwheels have been used to extract power from running water for more than 2,000 years. The force of the water moved blades, paddles, or buckets on the wheel to turn it. The turning wheel rotated gears and shafts, which in turn drove machinery, often turning the grinding stones in flour mills such as this one. Simple wheels varied in speed according to the water flow rate. More sophisticated waterwheels provided consistent power because they were driven by the weight of water stored in a reservoir.

JAMES WATT
The first steam engines were clumsy devices with pistons that moved in and out with a slow, jerky action. They were fine for pumping water, but they could not turn a rotating shaft. In 1765 the Scottish engineer James Watt invented a new type of steam engine with a smooth, continuous action that could be used as a power source for heavy industry. It was also ideal for driving steam railroad locomotives.

STEAM PRESSURE
Old railroad engines such as this are driven by steam pressure that builds up when burning coal heats water in an enclosed boiler. The same principle is used to drive fanlike turbines in power plants to generate electricity. The heat that turns the water to steam can be produced by a furnace that burns fuel such as coal or gas, or by a nuclear reactor. Some turbines even run on steam that is generated by solar energy.

46512

60 B

THE STRATHSPEY CLANSMAN

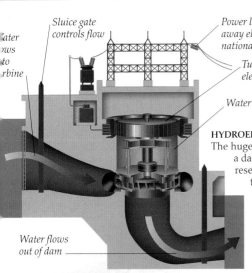

Sluice gate controls flow

Power lines carry away electricity to national grid

Turbine turns electricity generator

Water pressure spins turbine

ater ws to rbine

Water flows out of dam

HYDROELECTRICITY

The huge weight of water behind a dam that holds back a reservoir can provide energy to make electricity. The water pressure spins the blades of big turbines that are built into tunnels passing through the dam, and these turbines turn the generators that produce electricity.

TIDAL SURGE

Barrages built across tidal river estuaries generate electricity in a similar way to hydroelectric plants. As the tide rises and falls it flows through turbines built into the barrage, and these drive electricity generators. The system can work well, but such barrages can upset the balance of nature in estuaries by disrupting the rhythm of the tides.

Rising and falling water surge acts as a pump

Air pressure drives turbine and generator

Diagram of LIMPET

Waves cause surge of water in and out of plant

WAVE POWER

Ocean waves have the power to bring down cliffs and sink ships, but this energy is difficult to turn into electricity. One system than can harness wave energy and generate electricity from it is the Land Installed Marine Power Energy Transmitter (LIMPET) on the island of Islay off Scotland, UK. The system creates electricity with turbines powered by the air pressure built up by waves surging in and out of a concrete chamber.

Tower anchors the turbine and acts as a warning beacon for ships

Rotating turbine blades drive generators

OCEAN CURRENTS

Systems are being designed to harness the colossal power of ocean currents. The Gulf Stream current in the Atlantic Ocean flows swiftly and strongly between Florida and the nearby Bahamas. Here there are plans to install a series of submerged, anchored turbines that will drive electricity generators. The designers believe that these could produce as much electricity as a nuclear power plant—but with none of the dangers or potential pollution problems.

Water conflict

WE TAKE CLEAN WATER for granted. But in many parts of the world, fresh water is a luxury. It is so scarce and so valuable that people regularly risk their lives to gain access to it. In these regions extracting water from rivers for farming and city use can cause serious problems for people living downstream, as can damming rivers to provide power. The pollution of streams and rivers can have disastrous impacts on wildlife. All these problems can lead to political conflict and, if they are serious enough, can even trigger wars.

VITAL SOURCE
Only 10 percent of the world's population have tap water in their homes. The rest must carry their water from communal sources. For these people, every drop of water is precious. They would never dream of wasting water, because they have barely enough for their needs.

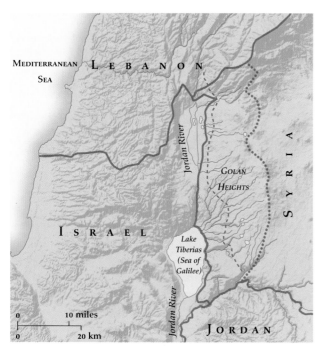

WATER WARS
Disputes over water supply can lead to bitter conflict. In the early 1960s, Syria tried to divert water draining off the Golan Heights toward neighboring Israel by building a canal, shown as a blue dashed line on this map. The Israelis forced the Syrians to abandon the project, but tensions over water resources escalated into the Six-Day War in 1967, when Israel invaded Syria. Israel went on to occupy the entire Golan Heights region up to the dotted purple line, controlling all the water draining off the high land. Israel continues to occupy the Golan Heights and this is still an issue in Middle-Eastern politics today.

Sheet of Libyan stamps commemorating the Great Manmade River project

WASTING WATER
We waste water without thinking about it. Some 30 percent of the water we use in the home is flushed down the toilet. We use even more to wash cars and sprinkle lawns to keep them green in summer. We even waste water in semideserts such as the one surrounding Las Vegas, where vast quantities of water are used to create golf courses like this one.

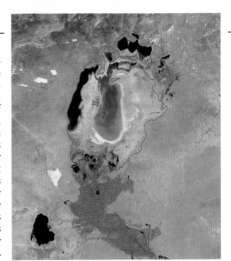

DIVERTING RIVERS
Channelling water into irrigation programs can have disastrous effects. In the 1960s, 90 percent of the water that had been flowing into the Aral Sea in northwestern Asia was redirected into irrigation for growing cotton. As a result the Aral Sea shrunk from its original extent, marked by the red line on this satellite image, to one-tenth of its former size, and the lake's water became intensely salty and polluted.

Colonel Gadaffi, Libya's leader

DRAINING THE DESERT
The Great Manmade River project in Libya, north Africa, draws water from a natural reservoir beneath the Sahara that accumulated during the last glacial period, which ended about 20,000 years ago. The program is supplying vast amounts of water each day to the major cities of Libya and has won Libyan politicians short-term prestige. But the water is not being replaced, so it will eventually run out. This could lead to many oases and towns in the desert losing their vital water supplies.

Huge concrete pipes for the Great Manmade River are hoisted into place by cranes

Stamps show how water will be used to grow crops in the desert

WATER POLLUTION
Mining and industrial waste dumped in rivers can poison the river or restrict its flow, killing the wildlife and destroying the livelihoods of people living downstream. Pollution also affects the oceans. Some is deliberate, such as dumping at sea, but accidents such as oil spills can be just as devastating to animals such as this penguin. The coastal communities affected by these environmental disasters are often not properly compensated.

THINK BEFORE YOU DRINK!
Every year manufacturers use about 2.7 million tons of plastic to bottle water. Most of those bottles are produced from crude oil, a nonrenewable resource. Almost 90 percent of the plastic bottles end up in landfill sites, where they can take up to 1,000 years to break down. Despite these environmental concerns, in parts of the world where clean drinking water is not available, bottled water is often the only safe option.

CLIMATE CHANGE
We are facing the probability of dramatic climate change. This is likely to cause more intense storms and local flooding in some areas, while others will suffer prolonged droughts that create deserts and trigger catastrophic fires like this. Such events, caused entirely by too much or too little water, will have big political impacts as national economies suffer and people migrate to regions that are not so badly affected.

Water in the future

WATER IS GOING TO PLAY an increasingly important part in the future of humanity. As human populations grow, and some areas become affected by droughts caused by climate change, water supplies may become stretched to the limit. We are already finding new sources of water, however, and finding ways to avoid waste and make the best of the water resources we already have. Before long, water conservation and recycling systems will be built into every new home, office, school, and factory, and efficient ways of using water will become part of everyday life.

THE VALUE OF WATER
In the past, life-giving fresh water was often seen as an almost sacred substance, and was frequently used to enhance temples and other places of deep spiritual significance, such as the Taj Mahal in India. Today many people have lost that sense of the value of water, but we must get it back if we are to use water wisely in the future.

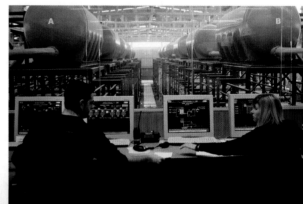

SECURING SUPPLIES
As rainfall patterns change, many countries may find that their water resources are inadequate and will need to search for others. One option is harvesting rain water or recycling some wastewater. Another option is removing salt from seawater, here being directed from the control room of a desalination plant in southern Spain.

SIMPLE SOLUTIONS
Many organizations are working hard to improve water supplies in places where clean drinking water is a scarce resource. The Hitosa gravity flow project in central Ethiopia has involved tapping the water from two springs, and using these pipes to carry it downhill to 31 villages and towns. It now supplies some 60,000 people with safe water.

Rainwater drains off roof into gutter system

Low-flow shower drains into gray water network

Low-volume tub drains into gray water system

Toilet cistern supplied with recycled water

Water barrel collects rainwater, which can be used to wash car

Black water from toilet goes to treatment plant

Wastewater from dishwasher flows into gray water network

Sink drains into gray water system

WATER CONSERVATION
Some houses are now being built with water conservation systems. These systems can also be added to older houses. Used water (known as gray water) from bathtubs, showers, and washing machines is filtered and treated to remove pollutants, and mixed with rainwater from the roof. It is then used for functions like flushing the toilet, vastly reducing the consumption of mains water.

Gutter collects rainwater for storage

Drought-resistant plants reduce need for watering

Recycled water is used for yard irrigation

Rainwater is mixed with treated gray water in storage tank

Mains water supply is fed to faucets

Water meter on mains supply monitors usage

Washing machine uses recycled water

Graywater treatment tank removes soap and dirt

Pump sends treated gray water to storage tank

Pump sends recycled water to roof tank

WATER AND WILDLIFE
Droughts in the future could have dramatic effects on wildlife, especially the plants and animals of wild wetlands. Many wetlands are now protected wildlife reserves, where water levels are kept high to keep the ground wet. This ensures the survival of marshland and bog species such as these trumpet pitcher plants being examined by a biologist in the southeastern United States.

Amaranth plant

Amaranth grain

CROPS FOR ARID LANDS
Regions that become more arid in the future will need crops that can survive with less water. These include amaranth, a high-yielding grain crop that is far more tolerant of drought than most crop plants. The grain can be used instead of rice or wheat, and because of its high protein content it is very nutritious.

Access and consumption

W ATER IS VERY UNEVENLY DISTRIBUTED across Earth, with some areas getting regular torrential rain while others suffer years of drought. In general, people live in regions where water supplies are reliable, but rising populations and changing climates mean that many now have difficulty getting enough water. Nine out of ten people have to fetch their water from communal sources, and of these, about 15 percent are forced to rely on sources that may be unsafe. Better water-supply systems may improve these figures, but the improvement could be offset by population growth and climate change.

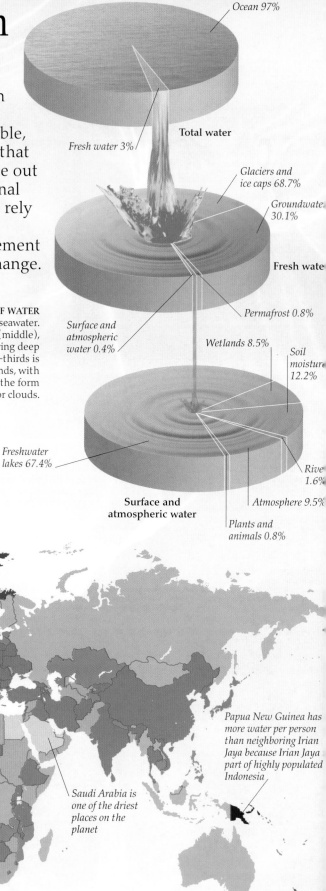

Ocean 97%

Total water

Fresh water 3%

Glaciers and ice caps 68.7%

Groundwater 30.1%

Fresh water

Permafrost 0.8%

Surface and atmospheric water 0.4%

Wetlands 8.5%

Soil moisture 12.2%

Freshwater lakes 67.4%

River 1.6%

Surface and atmospheric water

Atmosphere 9.5%

Plants and animals 0.8%

DISTRIBUTION OF WATER
Most of the water on Earth (top) is salty seawater. Only a small proportion is fresh water (middle), and most of that is either frozen, or lying deep underground. Of the rest (bottom), two-thirds is contained in freshwater lakes and wetlands, with far less in rivers. Almost ten percent is in the form of atmospheric water vapor or clouds.

WATER AVAILABILITY
The availability of renewable water to people in different nations depends on how much water there is in water sources, such as in streams or aquifers that refill from rain and snow, runoff, or groundwater. The availability of water also depends on how many people there are. Australia, for example, has vast areas of desert but a small population, so it has more water available per person than India, which has far more water but a much bigger population. Some desert states have so little water that they import extra supplies.

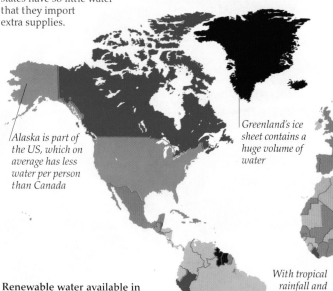

Alaska is part of the US, which on average has less water per person than Canada

Greenland's ice sheet contains a huge volume of water

Papua New Guinea has more water per person than neighboring Irian Jaya because Irian Jaya part of highly populated Indonesia

With tropical rainfall and a small population, Gabon never runs short of water

Saudi Arabia is one of the driest places on the planet

Renewable water available in cubic meters (264 gallons) per person per year

- less than 100
- 100–999
- 1,000–4,999
- 5,000–9,999
- 10,000–49,999
- 50,000–100,000
- more than 100,000

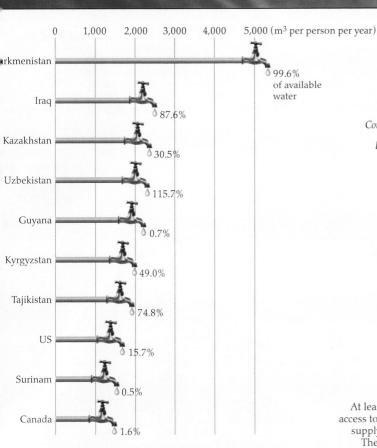

0   1,000   2,000   3,000   4,000   5,000 (m³ per person per year)

Turkmenistan — 99.6% of available water

Iraq — 87.6%

Kazakhstan — 30.5%

Uzbekistan — 115.7%

Guyana — 0.7%

Kyrgyzstan — 49.0%

Tajikistan — 74.8%

US — 15.7%

Surinam — 0.5%

Canada — 1.6%

TOP TEN WATER CONSUMERS
The yearly water usage per person often depends on the climate. Turkmenistan is a very dry area of central Asia where crops have to be irrigated, so it uses most of its water resources. Canada has a lot more rainfall, less need for irrigation, and a lot more water to spare. (One cubic meter / m³ is 264 gallons.)

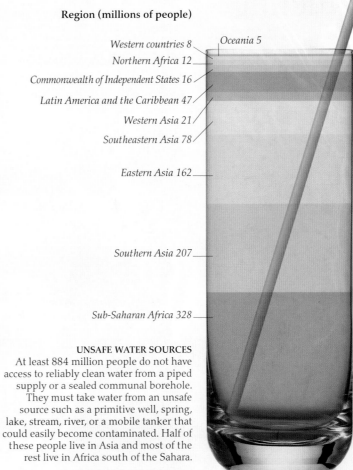

Region (millions of people)

Western countries 8 — Oceania 5
Northern Africa 12
Commonwealth of Independent States 16
Latin America and the Caribbean 47
Western Asia 21
Southeastern Asia 78
Eastern Asia 162
Southern Asia 207
Sub-Saharan Africa 328

UNSAFE WATER SOURCES
At least 884 million people do not have access to reliably clean water from a piped supply or a sealed communal borehole. They must take water from an unsafe source such as a primitive well, spring, lake, stream, river, or a mobile tanker that could easily become contaminated. Half of these people live in Asia and most of the rest live in Africa south of the Sahara.

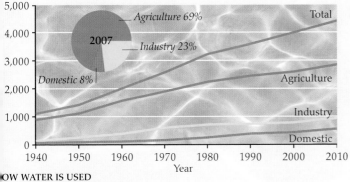

Agriculture 69%
2007
Industry 23%
Domestic 8%

Total
Agriculture
Industry
Domestic

5,000 | 4,000 | 3,000 | 2,000 | 1,000 | 0
1940 1950 1960 1970 1980 1990 2000 2010
Year

HOW WATER IS USED
Since 1940 the world's water use has risen steadily, mainly due to the increase in the population, greater industrialization, and more widespread intensive farming. Industrial use of water has increased more than domestic use, but the main consumer of water is agriculture. The inset chart shows how water was used in 2007—agriculture accounts for more than two-thirds of the total. (One cubic kilometer / km³ is 264 billion gallons.)

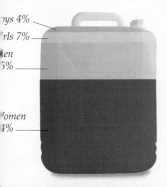

Boys 4%
Girls 7%
Men 5%
Women 4%

WHO COLLECTS THE WATER?
About 90 percent of the world's population must get its water from communal sources. Despite its weight, water is generally collected by women as part of their traditional domestic role. This can be a sociable task, offering the chance to meet and talk. Many women walk 10 miles (16 km) or more every day to fetch water.

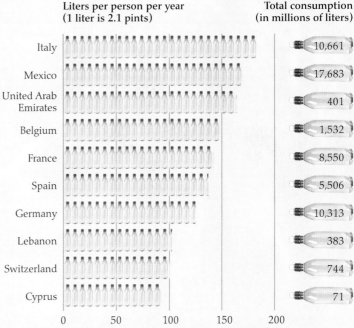

Liters per person per year (1 liter is 2.1 pints) | **Total consumption** (in millions of liters)

Italy — 10,661
Mexico — 17,683
United Arab Emirates — 401
Belgium — 1,532
France — 8,550
Spain — 5,506
Germany — 10,313
Lebanon — 383
Switzerland — 744
Cyprus — 71

0   50   100   150   200

BOTTLED WATER CONSUMPTION
The biggest consumers of bottled water, per person, are the Italians. But Mexico uses more in total because it has a bigger population, while the total consumption of the UAE is relatively small. Some of these countries use a lot of bottled water because they do not have reliably safe piped supplies. The US uses the most bottled water in total, consuming 26,000 million liters.

Timeline

Wₐₜₑᵣ has played a major role in history, in agriculture and technology, and in travel, exploration and trade. In the 17th century scientists began investigating the nature of water itself, and later discoveries helped explain the role of water in the weather, climate, life, and even global geology. Meanwhile advances in water treatment and supply have helped combat water-borne disease and pollution.

Grain grown by first farmers c. 9000 BCE

c. 4 BILLION YEARS AGO
The first oceans form.

c. 3.8 BILLION YEARS AGO
The first life forms develop in the oceans.

c. 400 MILLION YEARS AGO
Amphibians evolve from fish.

c. 2 MILLION YEARS AGO
The current ice age begins. Sheets of ice cover North America and the northern parts of Europe and Asia.

c. 50,000 BCE
First people migrate over open sea to colonize Australia.

c. 15,000 BCE
The last interglacial, or cold phase, of the current ice age ends.

c. 9000 BCE
Mesopotamians use irrigation to become the first farmers.

c. 1500 BCE
Polynesians start to colonize islands in the Pacific Ocean, crossing the ocean in large double-hulled sailing canoes. They reach Hawaii and New Zealand by 1000 CE.

c. 600 BCE
The Romans install the first large-scale underground sewer networks.

Isaac Newton explains tides, 1697

c. 312 BCE
The Romans begin to supply their cities with fresh water via aqueducts.

c. 985 CE
Vikings discover the coast of North America.

1492
Genovese navigator Christopher Columbus crosses the Atlantic and discovers the West Indies.

1519–21
Portuguese navigator Ferdinand Magellan undertakes the first voyage around the world.

1611
German astronomer Johannes Kepler is first to describe the six-sided shape of snowflakes.

1662
British scientist and architect Christopher Wren invents the first modern rain gauge.

1697
British scientist Isaac Newton explains how the gravity of the Moon causes the tides.

1735
British physicist George Hadley explains how water vapour circulates in the atmosphere.

1742
Swedish scientist Anders Celsius devises his temperature scale based on the freezing and boiling points of water.

Romans build aqueducts, such as this one in Segovia, Spain, from about 312 BCE

70
...merican inventor and statesman Benjamin
...nklin publishes the first description and map
...the Gulf Stream ocean current.

...68–79
...tish explorer Captain James Cook
...dertakes three voyages of exploration,
...inly in the Pacific and Southern Ocean,
...ere he charts many of the islands and the
...stern coast of Australia.

...83
...nch scientist Antoine Lavoisier shows
...at water is composed of hydrogen and
...ygen.

...00
...tish scientists William Nicholson
...d Anthony Carlisle use electricity
...split water into hydrogen and
...ygen gas.

...03
...tish amateur meteorologist Luke
...ward devises a naming scheme
...clouds.

...04
...e first citywide, municipal water treatment
...nt is installed in Paisley, Scotland.

...05
...nch scientist Joseph-Louis Gay-Lussac
...ows that water consists of two parts hydrogen
...one part oxygen by volume.

...19
...iss chemist Alexander Marcet discovers that
...e basic chemistry of seawater is the same
...roughout the world.

...29
...t James Simpson develops a water
...rification system based on sand filtration.

...31–36
...tish naturalist Charles Darwin conducts
...me of the earliest oceanographic research
...ring the voyage of the *Beagle*.

...54
...glish doctor John Snow contains a cholera
...tbreak by sealing a contaminated well,
...monstrating that the disease is
...read in infected water.

...MS Challenger

Newspaper reporting the
Chang Jiang (Yangtze
River) flood in 1931

THE ILLUSTRATED LONDON NEWS
SATURDAY, SEPTEMBER 19, 1931.
FLOODS IN WHICH SEVERAL MILLIONS OF HUMAN BEINGS PERISHED; HANKOW STREETS UNDER WATER.

1872–76
HMS *Challenger* makes the first thorough
scientific exploration of the oceans. The ship
travels 110,900 km (68,900 miles) on its four-
year voyage around the world.

1882
The first commercial hydroelectric generator is
built on the Fox River, Wisconsin, USA.

1920
Serbian scientist Milutin Milankovitch discovers
that regular variations in Earth's orbit around
the Sun cause cycles of changing global
temperature, which are responsible for ice ages.

1924
Russian biochemist Aleksandr Oparin
suggests that life on Earth could have
originated in the oceans. He says that simple
substances linked up to form the first
complex molecules essential to life.

1931
After three years of drought, the Chang
Jiang (Yangtze River) in China floods
and causes the death of more than
3.7 million people.

1932
After years of drought and
overcropping, the soil of
the "Dust Bowl" in the
American Midwest
starts to blow away.
The dust storms
continue until
1939.

1934
US naturalist Charles Beebe and engineer Otis
Barton make a world-record descent of 923 m
(3,028 ft) in a submersible called the
Bathysphere, pioneering deep-sea exploration.

1936
The first gravity arch hydroelectric dam, the
Hoover Dam on the Colorado River in
southwestern US, is completed.

1943
French diver Jacques Cousteau and engineer
Emile Gagnan invent the aqualung – an
underwater breathing apparatus based on
an air supply carried on the diver's back.

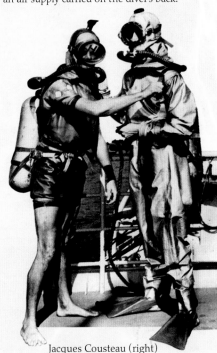

Jacques Cousteau (right)
and a diver test the aqualung in 1943

1944
The world's longest water supply tunnel is
opened, supplying New York City from the
Rondout Reservoir 169 km (105 miles) away.

1948
US oceanographer Henry Melson Stommel
publishes a paper explaining the workings of
the Gulf Stream and the ocean circulation that
redistributes heat around the world.

1951
Scientists find the deepest point of the oceans,
the Challenger Deep of the Mariana Trench in
the western Pacific. At nearly 11 km (6.8 miles)
deep, it is the deepest chasm on Earth.

1960
Jacques Piccard and Don Walsh descend to the
deepest part of the Mariana Trench in the
submersible *Trieste*, and discover marine life
even at this depth.

1962
US geologist Harry Hess proposes his theory of
ocean-floor spreading from mid-ocean ridges.

1967
La Rance hydroelectric tidal barrage begins
operating near St Malo, France, generating
240,000 kilowatts of electricity.

1968–69
British sailor Robin Knox-Johnston sails around the world to complete the first single-handed, nonstop circumnavigation.

1972
The US legislature passes the Clean Water Act to restore the chemical, biological, and physical nature of waterways damaged by pollution.

1977
US scientists in the submersible *Alvin* discover hot springs, known as hydrothermal vents, on the floor of the Pacific Ocean.

Robin Knox-Johnston on *Suhaili*, 1968–69.

1981
WaterAid, an international non-profitmaking organization, is set up with the goal of helping people escape the poverty and disease caused by living without safe water and sanitation.

1984
A long drought causes famine in Ethiopia and Sudan, killing 450,000 people.

1984–85
Work begins on the Great Manmade River project in Libya, the world's largest irrigation and water supply plan.

1985
Live Aid, an international rock music event, is held to fund famine relief in Ethiopia.

1985
The Dead Zone, a lifeless region in the Gulf of Mexico, caused by pollution carried into the sea by the Mississippi, is systematically surveyed for the first time.

1986
The world's longest barrier across a tidal river, the 5½-mile (9-km) Oosterscheldedam, is completed in the Netherlands. It is designed to defend the coast against very high tides and storms.

1991-92
Africa suffers its worst dry spell of the 20th century when 2.6 million sq miles (6.7 million sq km) are affected by drought.

1994
The UN Law of the Sea comes into force, governing how nations should safeguard the oceans. The law replaces conventions defining national rights over the seas that had existed since the 17th century.

1995
The largest ocean wave ever recorded strikes the liner *Queen Elizabeth II* off the coast of Newfoundland, Canada. The wave is 100 ft (30 m) high. Higher waves may occur in the Southern Ocean, but have not been measured.

2000
NASA's *Galileo* mission provides evidence that Europa, one of the moons of Jupiter, may have oceans of liquid water beneath its icy surface. If so, this would be the only other body in the solar system that has oceans—and it is just possible that these could contain forms of life.

2000
Research shows that, in less developed countries, 27 percent of the population (nearly 900 million people) do not have access to safe drinking water.

Galileo finds evidence of water on Europa in 2000

2002
A huge block of Antarctic ice that projects out to sea, called the Larsen-B ice shelf, disintegrates and 1,254 sq miles (3,250 sq km) of ice drift away in the sea.

2003
The world's first open-sea tidal power generator is installed off the coast of north Devon in southern England.

2005
An international team of oceanographers reports that the oceans are becoming dangerously acidified by carbon dioxide absorbed from the air. This could have severe consequences for marine life.

2005
A series of tsunamis, triggered by an earthquake in the Indian Ocean, kills about 300,000 people in Asia.

2005
The world's largest desalination plant for turning seawater into drinking water opens at Ashkelon in Israel.

2006
A scientific study finds that fish stocks have collapsed in nearly one-third of sea fisheries, and the rate of decline is accelerating. If the trend continues, many of the fish we eat will be too scarce to be caught by 2050.

2007
UNESCO declares 2008 International Year of Sanitation.

Hydrothermal vents are discovered in 1977

Find out more

WATER IS AN AMAZING SUBSTANCE, and there are many ways of exploring its different aspects. One of the most enjoyable is just to experience it in all its force and majesty on rivers, lakes, and the ocean. You can also visit nature reserves and aquariums to see how wildlife interacts with water. Museum exhibitions and displays at water engineering sites show how we use water in different ways. You can also think about how you use water yourself, and whether you might use too much in a world where water is precious.

USEFUL WEBSITES

- These four sites all offer good overviews of water:
  http://ga.water.usgs.gov/edu/
  http://library.thinkquest.org/C0115522/
  http://www.ec.gc.ca/water/en/nature/e_nature.htm
  http://www.allaboutwater.org
- This website, run by the United States Geological Survey (USGS), is all about the water cycle:
  http://ga.water.usgs.gov/edu/followdrip.html
- The Franklin Institute has an excellent website giving information about water in cities:
  http://www.fi.edu/city/water
- The US government's Energy Information Administration tells you all you need to know about hydropower on this site:
  http://www.eia.doe.gov/kids/energyfacts/sources/renewable/water.html
- WaterAid has a useful site covering access to clean water, sanitation, and hygiene education:
  http://www.wateraid.org/uk/learn_zone/
- The United Nations Food and Agriculture Organization provides water access and consumption data by country and by region on this useful site:
  http://www.fao.org/nr/water/aquastat/main/index.stm
- The National Maritime Museum of the United Kingdom has a site containing information on everything from maritime maps and charts to navigation instruments and sea-going vessels:
  http://www.nmm.ac.uk

EXPLORE THE NATURAL WORLD
Rivers, wetlands, and seashores are wonderful places to discover aquatic plants and animals and find out how important water is to the natural world. Guided trips are best, because the guides know what to look for and can identify most of the wildlife. A well organized trip is also the safest way of getting close to wildlife on the water.

Children bird-watching from a boat, Estrella River, Costa Rica

AQUARIUMS
A modern aquarium can provide a dramatic insight into what life is like underwater. Many, like this one, have glass tunnels that allow you to walk through the aquarium itself, and watch sharks and other fish swim over your head. Since water covers two-thirds of the planet, this is like seeing how most of life on Earth exists. It can be a memorable, magical experience.

WATER ENGINEERING
Some of the most awe-inspiring of all engineering works are designed to harness the power of water, or defend against it. Many hydroelectric plants run regular tours, and big dams can often be visited at any time. This one even has a public viewing platform overlooking the spectacular outfall.

Glossary

ACID
A chemical, usually liquid, that contains hydrogen and is able to eat away alkaline substances such as limestone.

ALGAE
Plantlike organisms, often microscopic, that are able to make food using the energy of sunlight.

ALKALINE
The opposite of acid. When acids and alkalis are mixed, they neutralize each other.

ANTICYCLONE
A type of weather system in which cool air is sinking and swirling outward at ground or sea level, creating high atmospheric pressure.

AQUATIC
Describes plants or animals that live in water.

AQUIFER
A layer of rock that holds water.

ATMOSPHERE
The layers of gas that surround Earth, held by gravity.

ATOM
The smallest particle of a substance. Elements such as oxygen contain just one kind of atom. Compounds such as water contain more than one kind of atom.

BACTERIA
Microscopic organisms with a simple single-celled structure.

BOILING POINT
The temperature at which a liquid turns to a vapor.

BOREHOLE
A type of well drilled deep into the ground and equipped with a pump for drawing up water.

CARBOHYDRATES
Energy-rich substances, such as sugars and starch, made by some living things and used as food.

CARBONATE
A mineral containing carbon and oxygen.

CARBON DIOXIDE
A colorless gas formed when carbon combines with oxygen. Living things such as plants and algae combine it with water to make food.

CELL
The smallest unit of a living thing, with a cell membrane enclosing liquids, nutrients, and organic molecules such as proteins.

CLIMATE
The average weather in a region.

Model of a cell

CLIMATE CHANGE
When Earth's climate is significantly altered because of natural causes or human activities.

CONDENSE
To turn from a gas to a liquid.

CONTAMINATED
Containing impurities and/or pathogens (disease organisms).

CONVECTION
The movement and circulation of gases and liquids in response to heat.

CURRENT
A flow of ocean water, driven by the wind or by differences in water density caused by temperature and/or salt content.

CYCLONE
A weather system with clouds, rain, and strong winds caused by air swirling into a region of rising warm, moist air.

DENSITY
The compactness of the molecules in a substance. Density gives the substance its heaviness. Icebergs float on water because the ice is less dense than the water.

DESALINATION
Removing the salt from seawater so it can be used for drinking or crop irrigation.

DEVELOPED COUNTRY
An industrialized and modernized country with a high level of income per person.

DEVELOPING COUNTRY
A nonindustrialized country with a low level of income per person.

DISSOLVE
Disperse a substance in a liquid so completely that all its molecules are separated.

DROUGHT
A long period with no rain.

ECOSYSTEM
An interacting community of living things in their environment.

EROSION
Wearing away, usually by natural forces such as wind, rain, or waves on the shore.

EVAPORATE
To turn from a liquid to a gas.

EVAPORITE
The substance left behind, such as s[ ] crystals, when the water in a solutio[ ] evaporates.

FLASH FLOOD
A flood that rises very quickly afte[ ] a rainstorm, and may form a stro[ ] torrent.

FREEZING POINT
The temperature at which a liquid freezes to become a solid.

FRESHWATER
Water containing low concentrations of dissolved salts, such as rain, rivers, ponds and most lakes.

GLACIER
A riverlike mass of ice that is flowing very slowly downhill.

Iceberg

GYRE
A circular system of ocean currents.

HYDRATED
Having had water added.

HYDRAULIC
Using water as a pumping fluid, but also systems that use oil instead of water.

HYDROGEN
The lightest gas in the universe, and a component of water.

ICE AGE
One of several periods in Earth's history when much of the planet was covered by vast sheets of ice. Each ice age had cold phases and warmer phases.

ICEBERG
Part of a glacier or ice sheet that has broken off and floated out to sea.

ICE SHEET
A thick layer of ice that covers a very large area, such as Antarctica.

IMPERMEABLE
Describes a substance that forms a barrier against liquids and gases.

IRRIGATION
The regular watering of crops.

LAVA
Molten rock that erupts from volcanoes.

MANTLE
The thick layer of very hot, but not molten, rock beneath Earth's crust.

MICROBE
A microscopic living thing.

MICROSCOPIC
Visible only under a microscope.

MOLECULE
A group of atoms held together by chemical bonds. A water molecule (H_2O) is composed of two hydrogen atoms and one oxygen atom.

MONSOON
A seasonal change of wind that affects the weather, especially in tropical regions where it causes wet and dry seasons.

NUTRIENTS
Substances that living things need to build their tissues or fuel and maintain their bodies.

OASIS
A small area in the desert that is made fertile by water that comes up from the ground, or underground water that has been exposed by wind erosion.

OXYGEN
An odorless and colorless gas with the molecular formula of O_2. Oxygen makes up 20 percent of the atmosphere and is a component of water.

PACK ICE
Thick floating ice that forms when the ocean surface freezes.

PATHOGEN
A microbe that causes disease.

PERMAFROST
Frozen groundwater that never thaws out.

PERMEABLE
Describes a substance that allows fluids and gases to pass through or into it.

PHOTOSYNTHESIS
The process by which green plants, algae, and some other organisms use the energy of light to make carbohydrate food (sugar) from carbon dioxide and water.

PLANKTON
Living things that mainly drift in the water, rather than swimming actively.

Plankton

POLLUTION
Anything added to the natural environment, usually by people, that upsets the balance of nature.

PROTEIN
A type of large molecule made up of smaller units called amino acids. Proteins are the building blocks of cells. They are involved in all life functions.

RESERVOIR
A water store.

SALTWATER
Water containing high concentrations of dissolved salt, such as seawater.

SANITATION
Facilities for dealing safely with sewage and wastewater.

SEDIMENT
Solid particles such as sand, silt, or mud, that have settled on the seabed or elsewhere.

SEDIMENTARY ROCKS
Rocks formed from compressed sediments.

SOLUTION
A fluid consisting of a substance fully dissolved in a liquid such as water.

Model of a stalactite

STALACTITE
A suspended pinnacle of rock in a cave, created by the dripping of water containing dissolved limestone. Formations created when the dripping water deposits minerals on the cave floor are called stalagmites.

STEAM
Very small but visible water droplets suspended in the air, caused by the condensation of water vapor.

STORM SURGE
A local, temporary rise in sea level caused by storm winds and low air pressure.

SUBDUCTION ZONE
A boundary between two plates of Earth's crust, where one plate plunges beneath the other and is destroyed.

SUBMERSIBLE
A craft designed to dive to the ocean depths.

SUBTROPICS
The regions of Earth that lie immediately north of the Tropic of Cancer, and immediately south of the Tropic of Capricorn.

SUPERHEAT
To heat a liquid such as water under pressure, so it gets hotter than its normal boiling point.

SUSPENSION
A fluid containing suspended particles of another substance that has not dissolved.

THERMOCLINE
The boundary between deep, cold, dense water and a layer of warmer, less dense water that floats at the surface.

TROPICS
The hot regions to the north and south of the Equator, between the Tropic of Cancer and the Tropic of Capricorn.

TSUNAMI
A huge wave generated by an earthquake on or near the ocean floor, or by the collapse of an oceanic volcano.

TUNDRA
The cold, treeless landscape that lies on the fringes of the polar ice sheets.

UPWELLING ZONE
A part of the ocean where deep water that is rich in nutrients is drawn to the surface.

VASCULAR
Living things having veins or similar systems of tubes for fluid transportation.

WATER TABLE
The upper surface of groundwater.

WATER VAPOR
The invisible gas formed when liquid water is warmed and evaporates.

WEATHER
The short-term conditions of the atmosphere at a given time and place. The weather is determined by such things as temperature, wind, rain and snow, and air pressure.

Tundra in bloom

Index

Acknowledgments

Dorling Kindersley would like to thank:
Hilary Bird for the index; David Ekholm-Jâlbum, Sunita Gahir, Susan St. Louis, Steven Setford, Lisa Stock, & Bulent Yusuf for the clip art; Sue Nicholson & Edward Kinsey for the wall chart; Stewart J. Wild for proofreading; Margaret Parrish & John Searcy for Americanization.

The Publishers would like to thank the following for their kind permission to reproduce their photographs:

(Key: a-above; b-below/bottom; c-center; l-left; r-right; t-top)

Alamy Images: Neil Cooper 52br; Marvin Dembinsky Photo Associates 63cr; Patrick Eden 52cl; Mary Evans Picture Library 67tc; Derrick Francis Furlong 19bl; Larry Geddis 20clb; Greenshoots Communications 53cl; Robert Harding Picture Library Ltd. 52tl; Israel Images 35t; Emmanuel Lattes 31br; The London Art Archive 56cra; Ryan McGinnis 13tl; Christopher Nash 12tr; North Wind Picture Archives 45tr; Vova Pomortzeff 39tr; The Print Collector 8bl, 9crb, 66tr; Magdalena Rehova 35c; Jeff Rotman 57c; **The Art Archive:** Bibliothèque Nationale, Paris 47t; Cathedral Orvieto / Dagli Orti 7cr; Rijksmuseum voor Volkenkunde, Leiden / Dagli Orti 54tr; **Sarah Ashun:** 12cl, 12c, 12cr; **The Bridgeman Art Library:** Private Collection 8c; **Corbis:** Christophe Boisvieux 34bl; Clouds Hill Imaging Ltd. 41tc; Dennis Degnan 69br; EPA / Shusuke Sezai 11br; The Gallery Collection 7br; Gallo Images / Martin Harvey 61c; Lowell Georgia 55bl; Mike Grandmaison 38cl; Hulton-Deutsch Collection 68cla; Amos Nachoum 15bl; Jehad Nga 50tr; Reuters

/ Ajay Verma 26-27c; Tony Roberts 60bl; Pete Saloutos 49r; Denis Scott 15t; Ted Soqui Photography 61br; Sygma / The Scotsman 57cr; Visuals Unlimited 44tl; **DK Images:** Alamy / Comstock Images 51bl; The American Museum of Natural History / Denis Finnin and Jackie Beckett 51ca; Dan Bannister 37c; The British Museum, London / Chas Howson 19tl; The British Museum, London / Geoff Brightling 2b, 70tr; Combustion 48cl; Courtesy of Denoyer - Geppert Intl 48bl; Donks Models / Geoff Dann 70c; Peter Griffiths and David Donkin - Modelmakers / Frank Greenaway 68b; Courtesy of IFREMER, Paris / Tina Chambers 5tr, 17tl; Courtesy of the National Maritime Museum, London / Tina Chambers 33cl; Courtesy of the Natural History Museum, London / Frank Greenaway 71tc; Stephen Oliver 4bl, 11bl, 57t, 57tl; Courtesy of the Pitt Rivers Museum, University of Oxford 4cr, 8tl; Rough Guides / Paul Whitfield 12br; Courtesy of The Science Museum, London / Dave King 11tr; M.I. Walker 40tl, 42c; Courtesy of the Cecil Williamson Collection / Alex Wilson 53tl; **ESA:** DLR / FU Berlin (G. Neukum) 6bc, 33cr; **FLPA:** Minden Pictures / Jim Brandenburg 38bl; **Getty Images:** AFP 36cla; AFP / Jose Luis Roca 62cra; Aurora / Ty Milford 70bl; Paula Bronstein 56b; China Photos 11cr; De Agostini Picture Library / Dea Picture Library 45tl; Discovery Channel Image / Jeff Foot 41b; Hulton Archive 37bc; Iconica / Grant V. Faint 62tl; Chris Jackson 28t; Minden Pictures / Foto Natura / Philip Frisforn 34cl; Mark Moffett 46cl; Photolibrary 55tr; Popperfoto / Haynes Archive 67cr; Andreas Rentz 11cl; Reza 60-61c; Riser / David Job 25tc; Science Faction / G. Brad Lewis 17t; Sebun Photo / Koji Nakamura 69bl; Stock Montage 58cl; Stone / Anup Shah 47tl; Stone / John Lawlor 9bl;

Stone / Peter Lijia 25cra; Time Life Pictures / Mansell 67bl; **Imagine China:** Run Cang 24br; **iStockphoto.com:** 15br, 23cl, 33t, 35bl, 36br, 53cr; Selahattin Bayram 64-65 (Background), 66-67 (Background), 68-69 (Background), 70-71 (Background); William Blacke 18bl; Vera Bogaerts 13cra, 71bc; Randolph Jay Braun 16bl; Elena Elisseeva 21ca; Michael Grube 45br; Brett Hillyard 21b; Marcus Lindström 49cla (Background); William Mahar 29br; Marco Regalia 16tl; Christopher Russell 34tl; Jozsef Szasz-Fabian 7tr; Evgeny Terentyev 3c, 10b; Edwin van Wier 42-43bc; **The Kobal Collection:** Warner Bros 20t; **Kenneth G. Libbrecht:** 3cla, 3tl, 3tr, 23cra, 23tr, 23tr (Insert); **Library of Congress, Washington, D.C.:** Utamaro Kitagawa 51cl; **Courtesy of Marine Current Turbines Ltd:** 59br; **Simon Mumford:** 60cl; **NASA:** 6-7tc, 26bl, 29cr; Goddard Flight Center Image by Reto Stöckli 35br; Image Courtesy GOES Project Science Officer 26cl; Kennedy Space Center 68tr; MODIS Rapid Response Team / Jacques Descloitres 14bl, 27ca, 56tl, 61tr; MSFC 23b; **NOAA:** NOAA Climate Program Office, NABOS 2006 Expedition 39tl; NOAA's People Collection 27cra; **Image courtesy History of Science Collections, University of Oklahoma Libraries; copyright the Board of Regents of the University of Oklahoma:** 38tl; **Panos Pictures:** Tim Dirven 60tl; Giacomo Pirozzi 50b; **Photolibrary:** Animals Animals / David Cayless 69cla; Jon Arnold Travel / Jane Sweeney 29cl; Michael DeYoung 43tr; Robert Harding Travel / Angelo Cavalli 54-55b; Robert Harding Travel / Christian Kober 33b; Robert Harding Travel / Thorsten Milse 47cl; Imagestate / Ed Collacott 30br; Index Stock Imagery / Jacob Halaska 13b; North Wind Pictures 58tl; OSF / Colin Milkins 13tc; OSF / Richard Herrmann 43br; OSF / Warren Faidley

23crb; OSF / Willard Clay 32cr; Phototake Science / MicroScan 49tc; Picture Press / Thorsten Milse 30l; Stephen Wisbauer 4tl, 55cl; **Rex Features:** Sipa Press 28-29bc; **Science & Society Picture Library:** 22cl, 23ca; **Science Photo Library:** Tony Camacho 57ca; Christian Jegou Publiphoto Diffusion 40bl; Planetary Visions Ltd 1; Dirk Wiersma 37bl; **Still Pictures:** Biosphoto / Dominique Delfino 37tr; Biosphoto / Joël Douillet 32tl; Dennis Di Cicco 7bl; Majority World / Abdul Malek Babul 32bl; VISUM / Aufwind - Luftbilder 54ca; Gunter Ziesler 40ca; **Louise Thomas:** 47b; **USGS:** 16cr; **Courtesy of WaterAid (www.wateraid.org):** 62b; **Courtesy of Wavegen (www.wavegen.com):** 59c; **Peter Winfield:** 12bl, 14cl, 22tl, 29t, 39cra, 39crb, 49c, 53tr, 53br, 63tl, 64-65.

Wall chart: Alamy Images: Cro Magnon fcra (waves); **DK Images:** Pitt Rivers Museum, University of Oxford tr (ship); **Kenneth G. Libbrecht:** fbl (snowflake); **Panos Pictures:** Tim Dirven fbr (children); **Science Photo Library:** Planetary Visions Ltd ca (earth); **Louise Thomas:** crb.

Jacket images: Front: Corbis: Franck Guizion/ Hemis: tc; **Science Photo Library:** Kevin A Horgan: tr; **Getty Images:** Ian Cumming/Axiom Photographic Agency: b. **Back: Alamy Images:** Roger Przybys tr; **Corbis:** Lester Lefkowitz cr; **Photolibrary:** bl, tl; **Science Photo Library:** David Parker cl

All other images © Dorling Kindersley
For further information see: www.dkimages.com